The ARAB World Today

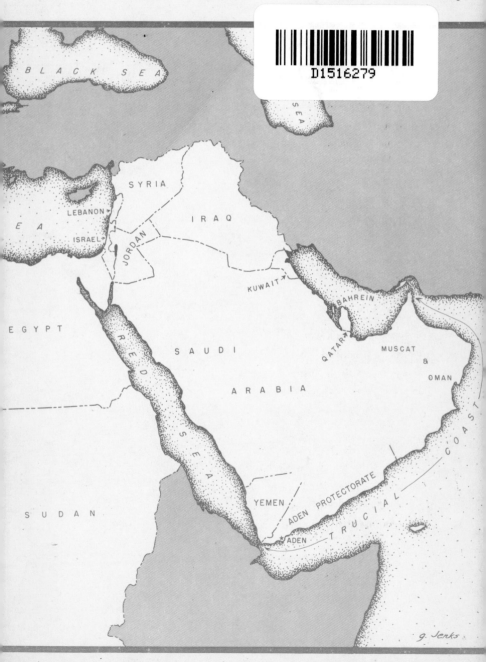

g. Jenks

The Crescent in Crisis

The Crescent in

Crisis

An Interpretive Study of the
Modern Arab World

by

Nabih Amin Faris

and

Mohammed Tawfik Husayn

UNIVERSITY OF KANSAS PRESS, LAWRENCE
1955

Library of Congress Catalog Card
Number: 55-7188

PRINTED IN THE U.S.A. BY
THE UNIVERSITY OF KANSAS PRESS
LAWRENCE, KANSAS

Preface

As we began this investigation, we had in mind a study of the unifying and divisive factors at work in the Arab world today. In the nature of the case, we were forced to investigate all those factors, the principal and the minor, the real and the seeming, the internal and the external. The investigation, therefore, became diversified, extending to a treatment of almost all the basic forces in the Arab world the existence of which strengthens one factor or another, unifying or divisive. This has made the work, in spite of its brevity, an interpretive study of all the problems of the Arab world today: the political, economic, social, cultural, and national. Whenever it seemed necessary, problems have been traced to their historical origin, and their relation to the other problems has been set forth.

In embarking on this study we made the effort to detach ourselves from ideas formerly held, in order to let the facts of the situation lead us to their logical and inevitable conclusions. It was not our purpose to promote any one idea, or advance any one principle, or side with any one cause against another. Rather, it was our purpose to try to depict the problems of the Arab world as they really are, and to place each accurately in its context.

In treating of the problems of the Arab world and of Arab nationalism, we did not proceed from abstract ideas and theories. Rather our starting point, and the axis around which the entire investigation revolved, was *homo Arabicus* as an individual possessing his own human personality and dignity, and as a member of a segment of mankind which has its own distinctive characteristics. Nationalism has never in our mind had legitimate claims which rise above those of individuals. It is rather the distilled essence of the characteristics of those individuals, and a program embodying everything that will lead to their well-being and happiness, and that will preserve their dignity as individuals, as groups, and as a whole people living in a fatherland.

The subject under discussion is not novel. Other writers and thinkers have addressed themselves to it since the dawn of the modern Arab awakening, and still do. What is possibly novel in this investigation is the analytical treatment of the subject and its comprehensive scope. In preparing this book we have made use of the works of hundreds of other writers, reference to some of whom has been made in the footnotes. To all of them we give our thanks and acknowledge our indebtedness. But our main dependence has been on direct study of the Arab world. This is possibly the first Arab attempt at self-examination and self-criticism, and the first comprehensive interpretation of the living Arabs.

This study would not have been possible without the generous support of The Rockefeller Foundation of the Arab Studies Program at the American University of Beirut. We are specially indebted to Mr. John Marshall of the Division of the Humanities of the same Foundation for his personal interest and encouragement in directing our attention to a systematic study of the living Arabs. We also wish to thank the University of Kansas for freeing the present writer during his stay as a Visiting Professor, from normal and routine duties in order to complete the present work.

Finally, the present writer must thank Professor James L. Wortham, Chairman of the Department of English at the University of Kansas, for his painstaking examination of the entire manuscript.

The University of Kansas
Lawrence, Kansas
April, 1954.

NABIH AMIN FARIS

Contents

Introducing
the Arab World

I. Arab and Arab World

THE ARAB WORLD consists of those lands wherein the majority of population is Arab. It extends from the Atlantic Ocean on the west to the borders of Iran on the east and from the Taurus Mountains and the southern shores of the Mediterranean Sea on the north to the Indian Ocean and the steppes of central Africa on the south. It includes Morocco, Algeria, Tunisia, Libya, Egypt, the Anglo-Egyptian Sudan, geographic Syria (Syria, Lebanon, Palestine, and Transjordan), Iraq, and the Arabian Peninsula.

Who are the Arabs and why are they so described? Is it because of race, religion, or language? Or is it because of a common culture, mental make-up, or common social structures and systems? Or is it because of all these that they are "Arabs"? The meaning of the word "Arab" has changed and developed in the course of time, and scholars, both ancient and modern, have disagreed on its definitive connotation.[1] In order to determine the current meaning of this word as used by the majority of those dealing with Arab national problems, one should know something of the development of the present-day Arabs.

From remote times, the Arabian Peninsula was inhabited by peoples belonging to the Mediterranean race. This group are characterized by long heads, brunet coloring, wavy hair, relatively small stature, and slight or moderate build. They have been called Semites. Some of them lived in fertile territories, while others were roaming nomads. Whenever the meager means of livelihood in the Peninsula proved insufficient for their sustenance, the latter were wont to push into the Fertile Crescent in extensive migrations, settle among the native populations, and eventually become completely mixed with them. Among these migrants were the Akkadians. They went into southern Iraq and became intermixed with the Sumerians, thereby forming the Sumero-Akkadian civilization. Afterwards came the Amorites, who reached as far as northern Syria; then the Assyrians, who established in northern Iraq an empire the sway of which extended as far as the Nile. There were also the Phoenicians, who settled on the

3

eastern shores of the Mediterranean, and the Hebrews, who for a certain period inhabited parts of Palestine.

The Fertile Crescent was not, however, settled by Semites alone. This area has been from remote times a coveted prize for conquerors, and a veritable overland bridge connecting three continents. Its strategic position, as well as its natural resources, has attracted empire builders from all directions. The Sumerians from Elam, the Kassites from Iran, the Hittites from the Anatolian steppes, the Medes from northwestern Persia, and the Kurds from the northeastern mountains of Asia Minor, all have settled in one or the other part of the Fertile Crescent and have become intermixed with its people. So did the Persians under Cyrus, whose dominion extended as far south as the Nile Valley. The Persians were supplanted by the Greeks under Alexander the Great. Soon afterwards the territory was divided between the two contending empires, the Sassanians and the Romans, into spheres of influence, or of outright annexation, until the Moslem conquest in the seventh century of the Christian era. But the Crescent had already been Semiticized, even before the Christian era. The majority of its population has become in the main Semitic, racially, linguistically, and culturally, while the influence of the Persians, Greeks, and Romans was for the most part confined to the main cities.

At about the beginning of the first millenium B. C., a Semitic people, the Arabs, established their hegemony over the Peninsula, and from time to time continued to overflow into the Fertile Crescent. Some established states and developed distinctive cultures, like the Palmyrenes and the Ghassanids in Syria, the Nabataeans in what is now known as Transjordan, and the Lakhmites in Iraq. Some, on the other hand, continued to flourish within the Peninsula. Those migrations into the Fertile Crescent, however, were not extensive, and failed to leave any marked influence upon the majority of the population. In fact those emigrant Arabs adopted the Aramaic language and became culturally Aramaicized.

In Egypt, the ancient Hamitic population, which belonged to the Mediterranean race, became intermixed with elements

4

from the north as well as with Negroid elements from the south. The Sinaitic Desert was the bridge between the Fertile Crescent and Egypt. Nevertheless Egyptian contacts with central and North Africa were stronger than the contact with Asia. The northern elements were mainly the Greek successors of Alexander, who remained in the land for about three centuries. They were supplanted by the Romans, who continued to rule the country until the Arab conquest.

North Africa was mainly populated by Hamitic Berbers. Other peoples, however, settled there and became intermixed with the native Berbers. Of these we may mention the Phoenicians, who established there commercial colonies, the most famous of which was Carthage, not far from present Tunis. From about the middle of the seventh century B. C. Greek colonists made their way successively to the region of Barca, where they established a number of colonies, the most important of which was Cyrene. The Vandals, too, attacked Tripoli and occupied it for more than a century (A.D. 427-533). But the influence of these divers colonies was insignificant, being limited to the major cities on the coast. The country remained largely Berber.

The seventh century saw an event destined to have a far-reaching influence upon the entire North African regions from the Egyptian borders to the Atlantic, radically changing the racial make-up of the population. Mohammed and his immediate successors united the Arabs of the Peninsula, who swarmed out of their "island" to overrun the adjacent territories, and from there pushed on across these lands until their empire expanded, in less than a hundred years after the death of the Prophet, from the Atlantic to the confines of China.

The most important results of these conquests were social, religious, and cultural. The conquered peoples gradually came into the fold of the new faith—some for convenience, to escape the tribute and steadily rising disabilities imposed upon all non-Moslems, and to enjoy the privileges hitherto the virtual monopoly of Moslems who formed, as it were, the master race; others because they were only too anxious to be rid of sectarian persecutions resulting from ever increasing

5

schism within the Christian church; still others crossed the doctrinal line because of the apparent simplicity of the new religion, its nearness to the comprehension of the masses, its emphasis on the human affairs of *this* life, and its relative freedom from ossified rituals and abstruse symbolism.

But not only did the Arabs give the conquered people Islam: they also were able to melt into the Arab crucible parts of these people, almost completely, and to Arabize others up to a point. Through this Arabization the conquered people, or those of them who were Arabized, relinquished their native tongues in favor of the Arabic. As should be expected, they also adopted such Arab thought as was embedded in the language, and their way of thinking was to a large extent modified and often limited by its methods of thought and expression. Furthermore, these conquered peoples became gradually intermixed through intermarriage with the conquerors, adopting their social standards, customs, manners and ways of life, as well as family organization and system of government.

For varied reasons the process of Arabization was, however, not so extensive as that of Islamization. To begin with, the conquerors did not settle in the conquered territory in the same strength. In some parts, as in Syria (natural or geographic Syria),[2] for example, their numbers were great, and their subsequent intermixture with the native population affected the racial make-up of the area, stamping it indelibly with the Arabian characteristics. In the second place, the Arabians of the Peninsula were in constant contact with the people of Syria, even before the Conquest, as indeed they still are. The majority of the natives, too, were, like the conquerors, Semites. In the third place, the area remained for many generations the center of Arab rule and influence. For these reasons we find the present population of Syria closer to that of the Peninsula than to those of the other parts of the Arab world.[3] In Egypt and North Africa, the Arab conquerors settled in smaller numbers, while in the other parts of their far-flung empire the number was too insignificant to produce any noticeable effect upon the native populations. The process of Arabization was complete in those areas where the majority of the population was Semitic, while in those areas where the population was not, deep-seated racial and linguistic factors precluded its success.

The process of Arabization was not sudden, but took a long time to unfold. Arab influence in Barca and Tripolitania, for example, where the Berber stock was predominant, remained inconsiderable, especially in the interior of the land, until the eleventh century, when the North Arabian and Nejdite tribes of the banu-Sulaym and the banu-Hilal moved on from Egypt, where they had been since the Arab conquest, and settled in Barca and Tripolitania as well as in Tunisia. This rather late migration accelerated the process, Arabizing many of the Berbers and strengthening the Arab character of the population. Another factor in enhancing the process of Arabization in North Africa, particularly in Morocco, was the migration of many Arabs and Mozarabs from Spain after the destruction of Arab rule there.

Arab infiltration into the Sudan commenced shortly after the conquest of Egypt in the seventh century. But wholesale migration of Arab tribes did not come until the thirteenth and fourteenth centuries. The admixture of the Arabs with the Hamitic groups dwelling in the north and northeast of the Sudan, with the Hamitic Berbers who had come from North Africa, and also with the African Negroes, produced the Arab and Moslem majority of north and central Sudan. The Arabization and the Islamization of the Sudan was not completed until toward the end of the sixteenth century, when the last of the Christian Nubian states was finally destroyed.

The admixture of the Arabs with other peoples continued throughout the Arab and Ottoman rule. In fact the process continues even to our day. Into the Arab world came various peoples: Persians, Indians, Turks, Kurds, Armenians, Negroes, etc., who came peacefully as laborers, artisans, mercenaries, concubines and slaves, while others came as conquerors, like the Buyid Persians, the Seljuk Turks, the Mongols, and last but not least the Ottoman Turks, who ruled the Arab world for four centuries. Similarly, the Crusades, whose sojourn in

7

the land lasted about two hundred years, did not depart without leaving behind a racial legacy, clearly evident particularly in the Lebanon and Palestine. The meeting points and melting pots of the different peoples were the cities, the large cities in particular. For the most part, the interior remained immune, and its people, especially the Bedouins, kept their racial purity and characteristics.

Actually, the regions wherein the Arabs maintained their racial purity to any large extent are limited to the Arabian Peninsula itself. Even there, however, admixtures with other racial stocks obtained. The effects of Negroid admixture are evident in the Tihamah, the Yemen, and Asir, as well as in the southern regions of the Persian Gulf and south and southeastern Arabia.

The Arab world has always been a crossroads and a meeting place, in both war and peace, and a crucible wherein race, religion, and culture were molten. Though in its isolated fastnesses indigenous peoples, and, later, refugee peoples have held to their national, linguistic, and religious identities, these were and are minorities within the Arab majority.

To sum up, the following definition appears the most satisfactory: The present-day Arabs are all those who inhabit the Arab world, speak the Arabic language, take pride in Arab history, cherish the general Arab feeling, and share in the characteristics of Arab mentality, irrespective of their religious affiliation and their racial descent.

II. Natural Divisions of the Arab World

MODERN MEANS OF communication have done away with geography as the sole factor in determining political boundaries. Large political units are now able to unite within their borders regions otherwise separated by geography, climate, and other natural barriers. Rather than existing solely because of geography, a modern state finds its being by virtue of the common will of its citizens to live in one corporate state. This common will is further sustained by common material interests, similar mental outlooks, and common hopes and aspirations. Nature and geography, which hitherto all but enslaved man, have now become his subjects, harnessed by his mind and controlled by his skill.

But man's control of the physical world, including geography, has not been achieved uniformly in every land. Parts of the Arab world, in particular, are still denied the modern means of communication—quick, comfortable, and cheap— both internally between its various parts, and externally with the world beyond. The effects of geography are evident and strong. Consequently we still find in the Arab world outlying regions, distant and remote, reduced to provincialism in customs, traditions, and dialects. These effects are likewise discerned in the way geography has delineated tribal migrations, the way it has retarded racial admixtures, and in the various strongholds it has created, enabling various groups to preserve their peculiar racial, religious, and linguistic characteristics.

At this stage, and before proceeding to discuss the natural divisions of the Arab world, it is necessary to point out that there is no intention of expressing any opinion regarding possible future Arab political groupings or provincial tendencies, since these are beyond the scope of this study. The purpose, rather, is to describe divisions as they exist, in the hope that such a description may help towards understanding political division and social differences in the Arab world.

The Arab world forms an uninterrupted ethnological unit —except for Israel, which was artificially introduced. But this vast Arab world is not lacking in geographical barriers, the most important of which are the extensive desert sands that separate its parts and reduce them to provincial units, differing in relief, climate, flora, and fauna.

The Red Sea divided the Arab world into two main parts, the Asiatic and the African, linked only by a narrow strip of land, the Sinaitic Peninsula, through the edge of which the Suez Canal has been dug.

In the Asiatic part three regional units may be discerned. The first region is that of the Tigro-Euphrates Valley. It comprises the present Kingdom of Iraq and parts of northern and eastern Syria. It may be divided into two subregions by an imaginary line drawn from Hit on the Euphrates to Balad on the Tigris, and thence to Sa'diyyah on the Diyala. The southern subregion has fertile sedimentary soil but little rainfall and intense heat. The northern is made up of elevated lands ranging between 700 and 1,250 feet above sea level, and rising gradually towards the east and the north until they reach the Kurdish mountains in Kurdistan. This subregion has heavier rainfall than the southern, and its average temperature is lower in both summer and winter.

Next of the three Asiatic regions to be described after the Tigro-Euphrates Valley is natural Syria, the region bounded by the Taurus Mountains on the north, the Mediterranean Sea on the west, and the Syrian Desert and the Peninsula on the east and the south. Its western part is lined with ranges of mountains, interspersed with fertile valleys and plains. The most important of these ranges are the Nusayri, the Lebanon, the Anti-Lebanon, Mount Carmel, and the hills of Hebron. Between these ranges and the Mediterranean extend narrow maritime plains. In spite of the fact that this region is divided into small distinguishable subregions, it forms a unit from the point of view of its geological make-up, the uniformity of its climate, with abundant rains in winter and continuous dryness in summer, and the uniformity of its fauna and flora.

The two regions, the Tigro-Euphrates Valley and natural Syria, are linked by the so-called Syrian Desert, stretching along an imaginary line from the Gulf of Akaba through the Northern Jawf to Kuwait. It is a desert gradually rising in elevation from the south to the north until it reaches its maximum height between Rutbah and Damascus, thence gradually falling to the depressed Euphrates Valley. Its northern parts have scanty rainfall, averaging two to six inches annually, which bestows upon the desert a cover of vegetation for part of the year. Together with the many wadis which retain quantities of rain water in the dry season, it makes of those parts of the desert a camping ground for the various Bedouin tribes.

The southern parts of the Syrian Desert are traversed by two prominent lines of water holes or wells which have led to the establishment of routes running east to west across the desert. "One line can be traced north-westwards from Jauf along Wadi Sirhan as far as the Hauran of southwest Syria; the other from Karbala as far as Ha'il."[1]

The Syrian Desert links the southeastern parts of Syria and the southwestern parts of Iraq with the third of the Asiatic regions—namely, the Peninsula.

This Arabian Peninsula is a vast platform of about a million square miles forming geologically a complete structural unit. It consists of a single block of ancient crystalline rock, the surface of which is covered with sheets of later sediments, for the most part of calcareous series, or of sandstone. Complementing its structural is its climatic unity, characterized by a scanty rainfall, not exceeding an average of ten inches annually, and by temperatures, except in a few localities, among the highest recorded in the world.[2]

The Peninsula may be subdivided as follows:

1. The Interior Desert. This is a vast platform which slopes gradually from west to east. The elevated lands in its north and central parts are known as the Nejd, a land of barren wastes with scattered oases. It is cultivable wherever water is available. This area also has barren mountain ranges, the most important of which is the 'Arid, which extends from Wadi al-Dawasir to al-Qusaym, and the Shammar, which lies north of Ha'il. The most important peaks of the Shammar are Aja' and Salma, which rise to a height of about 5,600 feet. Between Nejd and the coastal regions of the Persian Gulf lies the Dahna', a barren and sandy desert, with an elevation averaging 1,300 feet, while the Nafudh, a desert of reddish sand blown into dunes, and of barren rocks, lies between the Jawf and Ha'il and links the Nejd with the Syrian Desert. South and southeast of Nejd is the Rab' al-Khali of the moving sand dunes. It is the most extensive barren desert in the world, its area being about a quarter of a million square miles. It is also the hottest. It separates Nejd from Oman, Hadramaut, Yemen, and Asir.

2. The Western Highlands. This portion of the Peninsula is made up of several ranges of mountains extending along the

western coast, from the Gulf of Akaba in the north to Aden in the south. The most important in the north is the Sarah, while the most important in the south is the Yemen. The northern parts are made up of barren black rocks interspersed with numerous wadis and small arid plains. Rainfall is meagre and the heat is intense. The southern parts boast of higher altitudes, milder climate, abundant rains, and fertile lands, since they lie in the path of the monsoonal winds. Stretching between these ranges and the sea is a narrow sandy plain of intense heat and humidity, arid and unhealthful.

3. The Southern Coastlands. These stretch from the Strait of Bab-al-Mandab to Oman, with a gradual drop in elevation from west to east. In structure, this region closely resembles the western region. It is made up of a basement of granite and metamorphosed series, overlaid by sedimentary limestones and sand, with massive basaltic intrusions and occasional volcanic cones,[3] and dry and nearly dry wadis. The most important of these wadis is that of Hadramaut. Its flora differs from that of the remainder of the Arab world, but resembles, in some degree, that of Africa and India.

4. Oman. This region lies in the extreme southeast corner of the Peninsula. In structure it is distinct from the other parts of Arabia. It is for the most part a high tableland of about 4,000 feet in elevation, separated from the interior by the Rab' al-Khali, and overlooking the sea on the Gulf of Oman from steep perpendicular cliffs of intense humidity and heat. Rising in the midst of the southwestern district is al-Jabal al-Akhdar, which ranges between nine and ten thousand feet above sea level. In the region of this mountain are various rivulets and wadis with abundant waters that make the area rich in cultivation.[4]

5. The Eastern Coastland. This extends from the Peninsula of Musandam to the Shatt al-'Arab. It consists for the most part of an undulating plain, diversified occasionally by low hills, nowhere exceeding 600 feet in elevation. The northwestern parts, near the head of the Persian Gulf, are sandy or covered by stones and scree, and abound with swamps. The rainfall in these coastlands is scanty, not exceeding the four-

inch mark annually. The heat is intense, and the land is barren except where there is natural water or artesian wells. On the whole, the eastern coast, like the western, is not navigable by large vessels.[5]

The African Arab territory is divided into two regions: the Nile Valley and North Africa, known in Arabic as al-Maghrib al-Aqsa (the farthest west).

The Nile Valley comprises Egypt and the Sudan.

Egypt consists of the narrow and fertile plains on either side of the Nile. It is divided into two natural regions separated by a line running south of Cairo. The southern region extending from Cairo to Wadi Halfa is called Upper Egypt. It is made up of the narrow irrigation land on either side of the river. Rainfall is scanty, and the climate is dry, with temperature reaching 107 degrees Fahrenheit during the summer months. This region is periodically scorched by the hot dry winds of the desert, known as the Khamsin winds.

The northern region is called Lower Egypt, and is formed by the Delta with its two main distributaries, the Rosetta (west) and the Damietta (east), together with numerous smaller streams. Rainfall in the Delta is more abundant than in the southern region (Upper Egypt), and the climate is milder. The northern parts of the Delta enjoy the temperate Mediterranean climate.

Included in Egypt is the Sinai Peninsula, the desert strip which joins the Nile Valley with Syria through Palestine, and with the Arabian Peninsula through northern Hejaz. Between the Nile Valley and the Red Sea extends a barren tableland upwards towards the south. The southern half lies between altitudes of 2,500 and 5,000 feet, and occasional peaks rise some 3,000 feet higher, the highest being Mount Catherine (8,660 feet).[6] To the west of the Nile Valley stretches the western desert, which links up with the Libyan desert, itself an extension of the Great African Desert.

The Sudan may be divided into two distinct regions, differing in structure, climate, and population, separated roughly by the twelfth degree in latitude north of the Equator. The northern region is distinguished by the fact that most of its lands are arid wastes, while the fertile and arable parts are confined to the vicinity of the Nile on either side. It is further distinguished by its dry climate and scanty rainfall, and by the fact that most of its population is Arab and Moslem. This region, and more particularly the northern part of it, is an extension of Upper Egypt.

The southern region is for the most part made up of extensive fertile plains of black soil formed during many centuries from the sedimentary deposits of the Nile. Many parts of the region are swampy, its rainfall is abundant, and its temperature is high. It resembles in its structure, climate, and vegetation the equatorial region. It is inhabited by African tribes, speaking various African languages and dialects, holding various primitive religions, and living under social organizations distinct from those prevailing among the inhabitants of central and northern Sudan. It is therefore possible to fix the boundaries of the southern Arab world in East Africa at the twelfth degree in latitude north of the Equator.

North Africa (al-Maghrib al-Aqsa) includes Morocco, Algeria, and Tunisia. It forms a structural unit. It is made up of coastal plains with rich soil, plentiful waters, and temperate climate. In width, it ranges between 80 and 160 kilometers, and rises gradually from the coast until it reaches the Upper Atlases, which are a natural extension of the southern European ranges. These mountains slope down abruptly into the Great Desert. The entire region enjoys for the most part the temperate Mediterranean climate.

What is known today as Libya, consisting of Barca, Tripolitania, and Fezzan, occupies a middle position between the Nile Valley and North Africa. In structure, economy, and climate, Barca is a continuation of Egypt, while Tripolitania is a similar continuation of Tunisia. The western Egyptian desert links the Libyan desert, which includes Fezzan, with the Great Desert, which extends south of North Africa. It thus becomes the chief highway connecting all these countries. They are also linked by the narrow coastal highway which runs along the northern parts of Egypt, Barca, Tripolitania, and North Africa, as well as by the Mediterranean Sea, the

14

waves of which crash against the northern coasts of all these lands.

III. Political Divisions of
the Arab World

THE ARAB WORLD today has numerous political divisions, varying in extent, form of government, international status, and progress.

The Asiatic part of the Arab world is divided into the following:

1. Iraq. It is located in the northeastern part. Its area is 116,600 square miles; its population 4,950,000.[1] It is an independent constitutional monarchy, a member of the United Nations as well as of the League of Arab States.

The Syrian Desert separates Iraq from Syria (geographic), which is in turn divided into the following:

2. Syria. It is an independent republic, a member of the United Nations and of the League of Arab States. Its area is 66,046 square miles; its population is 3,350,000.

3. Lebanon. It is situated west of Syria along the eastern shores of the Mediterranean. Like Syria, it is a republic, a member of the United Nations and of the League of Arab States. Its area is 3,470 square miles (government estimate, 4,000 square miles); its population is 1,300,000. To the south of Lebanon is Palestine, which has been partitioned between the Arabs and the Jews, but the territories of which have been divided, not yet definitely or legally, among Israel and Jordan, and also Egypt, which has control of the so-called Gaza Strip.

4. Israel. It is an independent republic and a member of the United Nations. Its area at the date of writing is 7,800 square miles, and its population 1,500,000, of which more than 85 per cent is Jewish.

5. The Hashimite Kingdom of Jordan. It is an independent monarchy and a member of the League of Arab States. Its area at the present time, after the annexation of 2,150 square miles of Palestinian territory on the west side of the Jordan,

15

is 37,900 square miles, and its population, including some 960,000 former Palestinians, is 1,350,000.

6. Kuwait. It is a sheikhdom under British protection lying on the northwesternmost coast of the Persian Gulf. It is bounded on the north and west by Iraq and on the south by the Saudi Arabian Kingdom. Its area, including the island of Bubian, is 6,000 square miles. Its settled population is estimated at more than 150,000.

7. Bahrein. A collection of small islands the most important of which are Bahrein (proper) and Muharriq. It is bounded on the east by Qatar and on the west by the al-Ahsa' coast. Its total area is 250 square miles, and its population totals 120,000.

8. Qatar. A small peninsula halfway up the Arabian side of the Persian Gulf, 8,500 square miles in area and with a population of 25,000.

Between Qatar and the boundaries of the Sultanate of Oman are the so-called:

9. Sheikhdoms of the Trucial Coast. These have a total area of 16,000 square miles and a population of 105,000. The Trucial Coast comprises the following sheikhdoms: al-Shariqah, Ra's al-Khaimah, Umm-al-Quwain, 'Ujman, Duba, abu-Dabbi (abu-Zaby), Kalbah, and Fajirah (Fujayrah).

10. The Sultanate of Muscat and Oman. It is situated on the southeast corner of the Peninsula, with an area of 82,000 square miles and a population of 550,000.

11. Aden Protectorate. On the southern coast of the Peninsula, between the Sultanate of Oman and the Aden Colony, lies what is known as the Aden Protectorate. It has an area of 112,000 square miles and a population of about 650,000. Administratively it is divided into two parts: the eastern, with an area of about 70,000 square miles, and the western, with an area of about 42,000 square miles. Each part is administered by a British agent responsible to the governor of Aden. The Proctectorate comprises over thirty political units, including Sultanates, amirates, and sheikhdoms. The most important are the Sultanate of Lahj to the north of Aden Colony, and the Sultanates of Mukalla and al-Shihr in the east.

16

All these parts of the Peninsula just enumerated, which extend along the shores of the Persian Gulf and the Arabian Sea from Kuwait to Aden, are under one form or another of British protection and control. Some enjoy the benefits of more or less modern established government, such as Kuwait, Bahrein, and the Sultanate of Oman, while others are in effect tribal units governed by their respective sheiks in accordance with Islamic law, custom, and tradition.

12. Aden Colony. This is a British crown colony lying at the extreme southwest corner of the Peninsula. It has an area of 75 square miles. Belonging to it, too, are the islands of Perim with an area of 5 square miles and a population of 300, the islands of Kuria Muria with an area of 30 square miles and a population of 2,200, and the island of Kamaran with an area of 22 square miles and a population of 2,200. The entire population of the colony is 80,800, of whom 58,500 are Arabs and the rest Indians, Somalis, and Jews.

13. Yemen. On the southwest of the Peninsula is Yemen, the Arabia Felix of antiquity. It is bounded on the south by Aden, on the north by Asir, on the east by Najran, and on the west by the Red Sea. It is an independent theocratic monarchy, a member of the United Nations Organization and of the League of Arab States. It has an area of 75,000 square miles and a population estimated to be between three and a half and five millions.

14. Kingdom of Saudi Arabia. This consists of all the parts of the Peninsula except those already enumerated. It includes the Hasa region (annexed in 1913), the Sultanate of Ha'il (annexed in 1921), the Hejaz (annexed in 1926), Asir (annexed in 1931), and Nejd. It has an area of 580,000 square miles and a population of about 7,500,000. It is an independent theocratic monarchy, a member of the United Nations Organization and of the League of Arab States.

The African part of the Arab world comprises the following:

15. Egypt. This is an independent republic, a member of the United Nations Organization and of the League of Arab

States. Its area, including the Sinaitic Peninsula, is 386,198 square miles; its population about 20,000,000.

16. Sudan (or the so-called Anglo-Egyptian Sudan). In theory, this is a condominium subject to both the British and Egyptian administrations. In actual practice it is under British administration.* Its area is 967,500 square miles, and its population is close to 8,000,000.

17. Libya. This is a federated independent monarchy in which three regions have been incorporated. These are Barca, Tripolitania, and Fezzan. The entire area according to the latest estimates is very little over 1,000,000 square miles, and the population is about 1,350,000.

18. Tunisia. This is a French protectorate, the government of which is headed by a native ruler called the Bey, while the cabinet is formed of an equal number of French and native ministers. Its area is 43,313 square miles, and its population is 3,210,000.

19. Algeria. Officially a part of metropolitan France, Algeria has an area of 851,075 square miles and a population of 8,676,000.

The last part of the Arab West (al-Maghrib), known as Morocco, consists of the following divisions:

20. French Morocco. This is a sultanate under French protection. It has an area of 153,870 square miles and a population of 8,300,000.

21. Spanish Morocco. This consists of two parts, the northern, with an area of 7,592 square miles and a population of 1,140,000, and the southern, with an area of 10,039 square miles and a population of 12,000. Both the northern and the southern are under a Spanish protectorate.

22. Tangier. This is an international zone with an area of 225 square miles and a population of 125,000.

---

*On February 12, 1953, an agreement between Britain and Egypt concerning the future of the Sudan was signed in Cairo. Through this agreement the Sudan, after an interval of three years, in which all vital administrative positions will be turned over to Sudanese officials, would decide its future course along one of two lines: some sort of link with Egypt or complete independence of both Britain and Egypt. Cf p. 158.

Unifying
Factors

IV. Basic Unifying Factors

THAT THE ARABS, as seen in the previous chapter, are divided among themselves politically, and scattered into more than twenty separate states is true, but many forces tend to unite them and may gradually make them into one nation. Most obvious, perhaps, is the common land in which they live, the parts of which are all connected, and are drawing more closely together, in spite of natural obstacles, through modern means of communication. Of the unifying forces, we may enumerate also a common language, a common history and mentality, an all-but-common religion, and common economic interests and other minor factors which strengthen, from day to day, the major unifying factors.

1. ONE LANGUAGE

Language is more than a series of standardized sounds produced to express human wants; more than a vehicle to convey and sometimes conceal meaning; more than a treasury wherein the cultural achievement of a people is stored; more than an anthology which preserves their literature; more than a mirror which reflects their highest hopes and aspirations; more than a permanent record of their civilization and a key to their prehistoric ideas and attainments. Language is all of these and something more; something relating to man's spiritual being. Above all language is both the symbol and the bulwark of a people's spiritual unity.[1]

The Arabic language has always been the most important effective unifying factor among the Arabs. It is the common denominator of all Arab countries and peoples, irrespective of their dialects. The Arabs in the Peninsula, Iraq, Syria, Lebanon, Palestine, Jordan, Yemen, Egypt, Libya, and the urban parts of North Africa, understand this language, enjoy its poetry, appreciate its proverbs, and relish its maxims. Through this language they address their God, bespeak their love, express their hate, shout their oaths, and dream their dreams. It is the first thing the individual Arab hears when he is born and rocked in his cradle; and the last to be uttered over his corpse when it is placed in the grave. Whatever differences may exist between one Arab and another in social status or cultural level, geographic environment and religious community, all exult in hearing the Koran chanted, the poems read, and maxims and proverbs repeated. In fact, advocates of Pharaonism in Egypt, Phoenicianism in Lebanon, Syrian Nationalism in Syria and at present in Lebanon, and narrow provincialism in every Arab country have used for the spread of their ideas, not the ancient Egyptian or Phoenician or Syriac, but Arabic, the same Arabic language which the masses understand and prefer to any other.

It might be said that the Arabs do not speak one language, that the people of one Arab country speak a dialect which differs from the dialects of the others. This is true. Likewise it is true that the people of each Arab country speak various local dialects. The dialect of the people of southern Palestine differs from that of the people of northern Palestine no less than the dialect of Palestine in general differs from that of Syria or of Lebanon. The differences which exist between the dialects of the people of Mosul and Amarah in Iraq, for example, are even greater than the differences which exist between the dialects of Palestine, Syria, or Lebanon. This, however, is not the whole truth. These dialects have not developed into independent languages with any basic difference in sentence structure and vocabulary. This is because the spiritual unity of the Arabs is intact, even though the Arab world has been divided politically. This spiritual unity, which stems from the Koran, remains the same today as it was in the heydey of Arab political power. The Moslem Arab (90 per cent of all the Arabs are Moslems) still chants his Koran five times a day in his prayer, while the Koran and the *hadith,* as well as the multifarious works which have been written in commentary on the Koran and the *hadith,* are still read in mosques and schools or conversation. Speakers and preachers still address the people on Fridays and feast days in the classical Arabic. Consequently, the masses have forever remained in direct contact with the classical language. This contact is further strengthened by classical Arabic poetry, the influence of which is far-reaching. It has prevented the colloquial dialects from developing into independent languages.

22

The resurgence of Arab nationalism has gone hand-in-hand with an Arabic renaissance. The emphasis placed on classical Arabic throughout this awakening has limited the divisive influence of the dialects. Even among Christians, who are not so much exposed to Koranic influence as their fellow Moslems, the situation is not different. The translation of the Bible, both the Old and the New Testaments, into classical Arabic has had a similar influence upon the Christian Arabs and has tended to obliterate linguistic barriers between them and their Moslem brethren. At any rate, there is no country in the world whose people speak a common dialect. What is more, there is no one town or city, or even village, the people of which speak one common dialect.

This living bond between the Arabs is growing from day to day as a result of the increase in the number of schools, the spread of newspapers and magazines, the advent of the moving pictures, the all-pervading influence of the radio, and as a result of the use of modern means of communication between the various Arab countries, and within these countries. The trend which set in at the beginning of the modern Arab awakening in the nineteenth century is still towards one common simplified language which might be called *Unified Arabic,* in which all dialects would gradually melt, thereby removing one factor of disunity among the Arabs.

2. ONE HISTORY

The second unifying factor is history. This includes not only events, battles, and biographies, but also Arab victories and defeats, joys and sorrows, traditions, legends, mythology, folklore, and even superstitions. To the Arabs history is not something past, remote, and dead which they could recall at will and forget at will, but something real. The Arabs live their history.

Although Arabs of today are an admixture of many people and races, history and historical reminiscences fascinate them. This history begins with the advent of Mohammed and his mission. If it is ever pushed further back, it begins with that

23

vague period which the Arabs are wont to call "The Period of Ignorance," which was a preparatory period to Islam. It ends with the decay of Arab power and the eclipse of Arab rule in the thirteenth century in the East and in the fifteenth century in the West. Arab masses do not know anything of the ancient civilizations which flourished in the Arab world before Islam, and know still less of the peoples who have built these civilizations. No one will ever find among the Arabs anyone who has heard or boasts of Hammurabi, Esarhaddun, Nebuchadnezzar, Hannibal, or Rameses the Second. But everyone knows something, and often much, about the Prophet Mohammed, 'Omar, 'Ali, Husayn, Mu'awiyah, Khalid, Harun al-Rashid, Saladin, and 'Antarah. Arab awareness of their history is the result of their consciousness of being Arabs and, at the same time, is a source of that consciousness. This Arab consciousness, despite the facts of differing racial origins, is sometimes expressed in the idea that all Arabs are descendants of one ancestry and that the blood which flows in their veins is one.

Arab history is a living reality in the minds of Arab masses because it and Islam are to them one and the same thing. Islam in the Arab world is likewise a living reality confronting the individual everywhere. It is seen in the awesome old mosques, from the tall and beautiful minarets of which the muezzin's call rings out with the name of God and His Apostle, calling the Moslems to prayer five times every day. It is also seen in Arab ruins and remains which have come down from the time when the Arabs were lords of their fate. The stories of the Prophet Mohammed and his orthodox successors, and of the lives of the great caliphs, the conquering generals, and the religious leaders, are on every tongue.[2]

Probably no other people lives its remote past as the Arabs do. They speak of the deeds of their heroes as though these deeds happened only yesterday. They disagree on points that were argued centuries ago by the companions of the Prophet and their immediate successors. They still flock to hear such folklore narratives as the Thousand and One Nights, the Life of 'Antarah, the Life of Saif ibn-Dhi-Yazan, al-Zir Salim, abu-

24

Zayd al-Hilali, and al-Zahir Baybars, as well as the campaigns of Mohammed and the conquests of his caliphs—for the most part, narratives relating to the ancient folklore and history of Arabs and their civilization. Many literate Arabs today read Arab history and Arab ancient literature as though they were current newspapers and magazines carrying the latest news.

In some respects Arab absorption in their bygone days tends to be a chronic disease. It stems naturally from the general misery of the majority of the people and the wretched social and political conditions since the fall of the Abbasid empire and the Arab states in Spain and North Africa. They live in their splendid past as an escape from the miserable present. Many modern writers have strongly criticized this Arab tendency and pointed out its dangers.[3]

The people of a single Arab country may indeed be influenced by historical events which affect their own country or city or the families, clans, and tribes to which they belong. History may at times have a disuniting influence through the controversies it raises, involving religious sects or tribes. But Arab history in its totality impresses the minds of the Arab masses. And herein lies the importance of Arab history as a unifying factor, creating among the Arabs a collective consciousness and making them feel that they are the heirs of one nation whose forefathers have co-operated in the creation and sustenance of Arab civilization. The modern trend is to take Arab history, with its various events and heroes, and with its account of the civilization which the Arabs, Moslems and non-Moslems alike, have created, as an inspiration toward better days in which the Arabs will emerge from their miserable present to a more prosperous future. At the same time there is a tendency to belittle past differences and to emphasize what all Arabs had and have in common.

The influence of older Arab history is further strengthened by the history of popular Arab movements and of the national renaissance in literature and sciences from the beginning of the nineteenth Christian century. Arabs are much influenced by the lives of outstanding historical personalities, whose example is often utilized by national leaders today for buttressing the feeling of unity. Similarly, the struggles of modern national leaders such as 'Abd-al-Qadir in Algiers, 'Abd-al-Karim al-Khattabi in Morocco, 'Omar al-Mukhtar in Barca, 'Irabi, Mustafa Kamil and Sa'd Zaghlul in Egypt, King Husayn in the Hejaz, and hundreds of other leaders and heroes who gave their lives for the independence of their countries in Iraq, Palestine, Syria, and Lebanon, fighting against the Ottoman Turks, the British, and the French, have become part of modern Arab history and tradition.

Side by side with this unifying history there is one which the advocates of provincialism are trying to promote through schools, newspapers, magazines, books, and other means of influence. This movement has become stronger since the partition of the Arab world into several states, and since the advent of ruling dynasties and powerful leaders with local ambitions. This provincial historical emphasis rests upon the events of each individual Arab country as distinct from the others, on the enumeration of the glorious deeds of the different dynasties, true and spurious, and in the attempts to show that the disagreements between these ruling dynasties are actually disagreements between the Arab masses themselves. These activities buttress provincialism and increase the factors of disunity among the Arabs.

3. ONE RELIGION

Islam is the religion of the overwhelming majority of the Arabs today. As such it is one of the most important factors of unity. Nevertheless, to say this is not to say that religion can be a sound basis for nationalism in its true meaning. The national bond is distinct from the religious bond. In fact it has supplanted the religious bond among many of the modern states. But Islam had and still has influence in bringing the Arabs closer together and in strengthening the foundations of Arab nationalism. Its importance in contributing to unity stems from its being considered by all Moslems as a complete system, supplying all the needs of this world and the world to come. It is a religion which determines the relations of man with his God. It is a social system which defines individual and family relations and personal behavior in daily transactions. It is a political system as well as a legal system, and determines the kind of state and the relation between the ruler and the ruled. It is also, over and above what has already been stated, regarded by its followers as a science and a culture and a history.

Early Islam as preached by the Prophet in the Koran and the genuine *hadiths,* and as understood by his Companions and their immediate successors, was originally not so comprehensive. But it became so gradually, and Moslems came to look upon it as such.

This change of attitude by the Moslems towards Islam is what really counts. For ultimately the conception the people have of religion and of ideals determines their thinking and directs their behavior, whether or not that conception agrees with the original basic teachings. Widespread similarities in the Arab world, such as the similarity of family organization, mentality, individual and collective behavior, are to a great extent the result of the Arabs' being Moslems and of their living within the social, political, and intellectual institutions of Islam.

The influence of Islam in unifying the Arab world is not limited to its making social and intellectual institutions similar. Its influence goes further, uniting the Arabs emotionally and binding them to one ideal. To many Arabs Islam has been the only substitute for nationality. The fraternal sentiment of Islam takes the place of the national sentiment. In fact, Arab masses in every Arab country look to the masses of the other Arab countries as brothers unified by Islam in the first place and by Arabism in the second. It was such fraternal religious sentiment which has for instance bound Kurdish, Berber, and Negro Moslems. On this basis, we can understand British attempts to prevent the spread of Islam to the pagan tribes of southern Sudan and the persistent efforts of the French to weaken Islam and its cultural ally, the Arabic language, in North Africa, particularly among the Berbers. These efforts are directed toward weakening the spiritual unity which binds these people to the Arabs.

To be sure, the multiplicity of religions in the Arab world, as well as the division of each religion into various sects and congregations, always disagreeing and sometimes in conflict one with the other, carries the germ of disunity. Similarly, the incipient political movements now active which are based on religion, such as the Moslem Brotherhood, are opposed to the idea of Arab nationalism. Although these movements may go side by side with national and reform movements in the struggle for freedom from foreign rule, they contain in themselves the germ of an inevitable head-on collision with national and reform movements. Furthermore, the rise of some of the Arab states on religious bases and the rise of the others on modern, secular bases are among the factors of disunity among the Arabs. Together with other factors they are a very important obstacle in the path of political unity.

4. ONE MENTALITY

The fourth unifying factor among the Arabs is the similarity of their mentality and temperament in general. Arabs differ little in their attitudes toward the various problems of life, and in their response to external influences. Whether they are Moslems or non-Moslems, they have the same attitude towards problems so various as the dignity of the individual, human effort, time, and women. They also differ little in the way they understand the concepts of honor and manliness, loyalty and generosity, hospitality and neighborliness, as well as other social values and precepts, which are the outward or the practical expression of their souls.

Arab mentality has become more or less uniform because of numerous and complicated factors which have interacted for many centuries. The most important of these factors is the similarity of the economic, social, and spiritual bases upon which Arab society rests. Since remote times, this society has been for the most part agricultural, organized along feudal, tribal, and religious lines. Religion, in its oriental connotation

—involving first and foremost belief in the unseen and surrender to fate—has dominated the lives of Arabs for centuries. Arab economic life rests upon agriculture and upon simple manual crafts* in settled centers and cities, where a powerful few, including strong leaders, tribal chieftains, and feudal lords, exploit the labors of the majority, made up for the most part of impoverished and sickness-ridden peasantry, tilling the land, reaping the crops, and threshing them with primitive and wornout implements which have not changed since the dawn of history. Furthermore, a large part of the population is made up of nomadic or semi-nomadic Bedouin tribes who are in constant and close contact with the settled inhabitants, particularly of the country, and who leave the imprint of their nomadic and tribal mentality upon the entire population. Likewise, the governments of the Arab world, with almost no exception, have always been either theocratical or despotic (if not both at once), controlled by a few strong leaders who employ lash and religion alike in ruling their subjects† and obtaining from them unquestioning obedience.

To these factors which have been instrumental in moulding Arab thought and thinking, directing their tastes, and implanting the patterns of the ideal life in their minds, must be added the influence of Arabic itself, its recorded literature and oral traditions and lore, its poetry, folklore, legends, proverbs, maxims, songs, and modes of expression. What is more, Arab literature in general is saturated with the all-important spirit of Islam.

On the other hand, the Arab mentality, which tends to unify all Arabs and make them alike in their basic characteristics, is not free from influences which have always tended to divide and to prevent teamwork and co-operation. Among the deep-rooted characteristics of Arab mentality is the blind

---

* Notice that the word for craft in Arabic is *mihnah*, a derivative from *mahanah*, i.e., abjectness and lowliness. This reflects the mentality of the bedouin who considers raiding and warfare the only vocations worthy of the nobility, while other vocations are despicable, unworthy of masters and conquerors, but belong to the vanquished and the weak.

† Notice again that the word for subjects in Arabic is *ra'iyyah*, a derivative from *ra'y*, "shepherding the flocks."

29

belief in the unseen, dependence upon fate, and surrender to the unknown. These characteristics are particularly dangerous when they prevail among a people in periods of political weakness, intellectual stagnation, and social and economic backwardness, since they tend to cripple their creative will, driving them to dream of past glories, oblivious of their urgent current problems.[4]

Another characteristic of Arab mentality is an extreme individualism, which limits the concern of the individual to himself and to his tribe, and prevents him from giving his loyalty to any other established authority, except under compulsion.[5] This individualism resulting from the deep-rooted spirit of tribalism and the prevailing feudal order, as well as from centuries of arbitrary despotism, drives the individual Arab to solitude and a type of isolationism, to fear of all strangers and suspicion of their intentions, as it prevents him from co-operation with others and stands in the way of any concerted or united action with his fellow men. It renders the individual and the group more provincial, quick to take part in tribal, partisan, or sectarian feuds without ever thinking of the greater national welfare.[6] Finally, a characteristic of the Arab temperament is the manner in which he approaches any undertaking in successive and isolated spasms rather than in a continuous and sustained effort and endeavor. For this reason the history of the Arab national movement has been the story of intermittent and violent explosions interspersed with periods of repose and inactivity.[7]

V. New Unifying Factors

The Internal Factors

THE FACTORS DISCUSSED in the preceding chapter are among the most important foundations of Arab nationalism. Alone, however, they have proved insufficient in uniting the Arabs into one cohesive political unit—a nation. Indeed, these factors alone are insufficient to bring the Arabs closer together in order to safeguard their interests and promote their welfare. In the present chapter, the new factors which have arisen in the Arab world, and which are at work strengthening national consciousness, fortifying the factors of unity, and transforming the spontaneous but vague consciousness of Arab nationalism and Arab brotherhood into a purposeful, enlightened, and profound national consciousness, will be discussed.

1. Schools

There are in the Arab world today two types of schools: the old and the new. The old schools are, as it were, petrified remnants of those schools which have flourished during periods of Arab glory. They are at present found in the culturally backward parts of the Arab world: in Yemen, Saudi Arabia, the Sudan, and North Africa, and, to a lesser degree, in Egypt and the other parts of the Arab world. On the elementary level, these schools are known as *katatib,* and teach their students the Koran, handwriting, and arithmetic, as well as some language and religion. On the higher levels, the most important centers of which are the Zaytunah Mosque in Tunis, the only indigenous educational center throughout the whole of North Africa, the Azhar University in Cairo, frequented by students from all over the Arab and Moslem world, and the various schools of Najaf and Karbala in Iraq, the cultural and religious centers of Shiism. these schools impart to their students a comprehensive and detailed religious, linguistic, and literary education. Both types, the *katatib* and the higher-level institutions, have been a stronghold wherein the Arabic language, ancient Arabic literature, Arab history, and Arab tradition have been preserved and transmitted to Arab youth from generation to generation. But these schools, by limiting themselves to the superficialities of Moslem culture and focussing the minds of their students on grammatical and literary problems, as well as on religious arguments and legal disputations, and by ignoring modern scientific subjects and refraining from the employment of modern methods of education and instruction, have reduced their generations of graduates to a class of people with superficial education, narrow horizons, stagnant minds, and traditional and reactionary outlooks.

31

Their graduates are removed from the actualities of modern life, oblivious of the needs of their Arab society as it wrestles with its manifold crises and faces its unknown future, and imbued with a consciousness more Islamic than Arabic.

More important in this discussion, however, are the new schools. These are the modern schools which made their appearance in Egypt at the beginning of the nineteenth century and spread half a century later, in varying degrees, throughout the different countries of the Arab world excepting the Peninsula. In so far as they have been imparting to Arab youth modern education and, regardless of some diversity, employing therein modern methods of instruction, these schools are among the most effective forces developing national consciousness and preparing the new generation for assuming the responsibilities of Arab liberation, progress, and unity. In so far as they use Arabic as the language of instruction, they help the spread of classical Arabic, thereby reducing somewhat the sharp differences among the various colloquial tongues. They promote a unified language, halfway between the classical and the colloquial languages, used in speech and in writing by educated Arabs throughout the Arab world. Similarly, by emphasizing the teaching of Arab history and geography, they inculcate a common feeling among students and acquaint them with fellow Arabs living in the various parts of the Arab fatherland. For Arab ignorance of other Arabs has been one of the most important divisive factors. Furthermore, in so far as these modern schools impart to their students modern culture based on science, acquaint them with the history of other peoples and explain to them the mainsprings of their progress, they have opened the eyes of these students to the deplorable state of Arab society, have loosened the fetters of tradition and fanaticism which have hitherto held the Arab mind in check, and have finally created in youth the urge to investigate and understand the social, economic, and cultural problems of their country; they have created a readiness to follow the example of progressive peoples and to adopt the methods these peoples have employed in their development. Actually, from the beginning of Arab awakening in the early nineteenth century up to the present time, educated Arab youth has been one of the most important instruments of liberation and reform movements throughout the Arab world. The calculated neglect of modern education by colonial governments, vested feudal interests, and reactionaries in general can be explained by their fear of the power of educated Arab youth. When people could not be kept away from the schools themselves, the enemies of education for the masses have attacked it by attempting to corrupt the schools and school curricula.

Nevertheless these modern schools have by no means attained their full development, and their influence is still short of expectation. To begin with, they are numerically too few for the needs of the awakening Arab world, where the majority of the people are still illiterate. In the second place, they lack uniformity in their requirements, curricula, methods of instruction, and standards. For the most part they are government-controlled, instilling in youth the spirit of provincialism through their provincial curricula, resisting ideas of reform, and preventing youth from understanding the vital problems of their fatherland, under the pretext of safeguarding the new generation against subversive ideas, irreligion, moral lassitude, and politics. Mention should also be made of the influence of some of those schools, founded and maintained by colonial governments and foreign missionaries, which spread confusion among students, weaken their national consciousness, and all but extinguish the flame of nationalism among them.

2. THE PRESS

The first Arabic printing press in the Arab world was installed in Lebanon in 1610.[1] From that date on, the press gradually spread to the other parts of the Arab world, until it became an integral part of Arab life in the twentieth century. To dwell upon the importance of the press in promoting national consciousness among Arab masses is superfluous. It is sufficient to point out that through books, newspapers, and magazines, the press was instrumental in bringing the Arabs to a realization of their present lot, after generations and even centuries of ignorance and stagnation. By publishing materials from the early Arab heritage, which enabled them to become familiar with their common history and literature, the press has indirectly helped bring the Arabs more closely together. More specifically, the press (daily and weekly newspapers and magazines) has revived the Arabic language by promoting a common, simple, and correct usage, without breaking away from the structure of the classical language but at the same time revitalizing Arabic by modern transfusions of vocabulary and idiom drawn from everyday life. The press has also served as a unifying influence through the emphasis it has given to Arab news and problems, and through its championship of all movements working for Arab liberation and unity. It has served, as it should, as a public school for the reading masses, supplying them with world information and directing their national efforts. It has become the means by which the currents of thought emanating from the minds of poets, reformers, and revolutionaries were transmitted to the consciousness of the people.

The printing press has been the preferred instrument of the pioneers of the Arab awakening[2] in conveying their clarion call to the otherwise dormant Arabs. It has linked all Arabs in sensitive appreciation of the same thoughts, the same feelings, and the same aspirations.[3]

The press, however, has not always been helpful to the Arabs, since it has often been transformed by colonial governments and local proponents of provincialism into an instrument of disunity and division. Just as the pioneers of Arab nationalism and the advocates of Arab unity and reform have used the press for bestirring the Arabs to "life, liberty, and the pursuit of happiness," the colonial powers and their agents have harnessed it for dividing the Arabs among themselves, spreading confusion and discord among them, and finally diverting them from the basic problems of their fatherland. The story would be neither complete nor fair if no mention were made of the Arab governments' suppressing the freedom of the press and all but strangling it through executive orders and arbitrary measures.* It is not strange, therefore, to see many of the educated Arab youth bewildered and confused, divided in their patriotic and nationalist loyalties.

3. THE RADIO AND THE CINEMA

In spite of its recent beginning and numerous shortcomings, the Arabic radio supplements the work of the press in the education of the masses, the awakening of their national consciousness, and the enlargement of their intellectual horizons. It keeps them in touch with political life and developments, and current events both within the Arab world and the world outside. The influence of the radio, however, is more far-reaching than that of the press, since the radio is better able to convey information to the masses, the overwhelming majority of which are still illiterate. It likewise complements the function of the press in promoting the use of classical Arabic and bringing it closer to the general public. In addition, the radio, by broadcasting from every Arab country songs, poems, plays, and debates, in the local provincial dialect of each, is helping to level the barriers imposed by the unfamiliarity of localities with the vernacular spoken in others.

This influence of the radio in promoting the classical Arabic and in lessening the differences between the various vernacular dialects is further reinforced by the cinema, particularly through its use of classical singing in its presentations. The songs which the masses commit to memory and sing in their various gatherings have, through inculcating a feeling of a community spirit and a common language, been one of the most effective instruments in welding the scattered and otherwise loosely knit Arab public together. Actually, the modern Arab singers, in spite of the enormous amount of trash their songs contain, have been greatly instrumental in bringing the Arabs closer together, though unconsciously, through unifying their tastes and conveying to them the feeling that they belong

---

* During the last days of the regime of Bisharah al-Khuri, president of the Lebanese Republic from 1943 to 1952, ten opposition newspapers were suppressed and their editors jailed, by executive order, within a single week.

35

to one nation indivisible—or at least preparing them for such a feeling.

Although the cinema industry is almost exclusively confined to Egypt, it has, nevertheless, indirectly been a means of bringing the Arab masses closer together, by bringing the various Arab peoples closer to the Egyptians, the largest single Arab group. The Egyptian cinema, which employs for the most part in both its dialogues and songs the more cultivated local dialect, has penetrated almost every Arab city, and has become for the general Arab masses, within the limits of their meager financial resources, their only form of entertainment. It has likewise dissipated the belief that the various Arabic dialects constitute a deep-seated and basic division among the Arabs, precluding any possibility of understanding among them.[4]

Needless to say, the Arabic radio could easily be a school for educating the Arabs by giving them the correct guidance they need, calling them to a closer co-operation in facing their common problems, and urging them to liberate themselves from the fetters of outworn traditions and institutions. Instead, the Arab governments have so far employed this magic wand to separate the Arabs and to strengthen the provincial spirit among them. The same thing could be said of the cinema and music, the importance of which in promoting Arab co-operation and unity is no less than that of the radio. But so far authors, producers, musicians, singers, and actors have been content with appealing to the baser instincts of the Arab public, thereby dulling their national sensitivity and diverting them towards the unimportant in this all-important period of their history.

4. POLITICAL PARTIES

Around the middle of the nineteenth century, several literary and secret political societies were founded in Beirut, all advocating the liberation of the Arab fatherland and calling for Arab unity. Most of the membership of these societies came from the ranks of the educated Arab youth, both Moslem and Christian. Their influence was soon to be felt among the educated classes, particularly in Syria and the Lebanon,* and they were to be a factor in the growth of the later nationalist organizations. As the Young Turks, after the coup d'etat of 1908, began to preach freedom and reform, educated Arab youth, including certain officers serving in the armies of the Sultan-Caliph, organized a number of parties and societies, the most important of which were Nadi al-Muntada al-Adabi in Constantinople (1909), Hizb al-Lamarkaziyyah al-Idariyyah al-'Uthmani in Cairo (1912), al-Jam'iyyah al-Qahtaniyyah (1909), and Jam'iyyat al-'Ahd (1914). All of these had a common platform supporting the liberation of the Arab fatherland from the Ottomans, the revival of Arab culture, the development of Arab nationalism, and the restoration of the Arab heritage and glory. A number of these educated youth and officers took part in the political movements which the Arab world witnessed during and immediately after the First World War. Some of them carried the national struggle through party activity, the press, and education, while others were content to occupy key positions in the different Arab states which were conjured into being by the mandatory powers after the end of the war.

Since that time the Arab world has witnessed the growth of political parties and literary societies and clubs, the main concern of which was to instill national consciousness in their membership and their sympathizers, instruct them in the affairs of the Arab fatherland, past and present, promote co-operation among them, and inculcate in them the will to unity. Some of these parties and societies called openly for the establishment of a united Arab state,[5] while others called for the establishment of a federal Arab state.[6] It must be noted, however, that the overwhelming majority of Arab parties, irrespective of their varied political ideologies and social programs, advocate co-operation, in one degree or another, among the

---

*In this study, "Lebanon" is used for the Lebanese Republic which came into being after the settlement of the First World War, while "the Lebanon" is used for the Lebanon proper, i.e., Mount Lebanon, which comprised an autonomous administrative district under the Ottomans.

various Arab states. In so far as these national parties and societies have produced a generation espousing the idea of Arab nationalism, striving for Arab liberation, and working for Arab co-operation and progress, they have been among the most effective factors in promoting national consciousness.

Arab political parties, however, have not yet found a firm place nor reached a strong position in Arab society from which they could control or direct Arab policies and achieve Arab national aspirations. The reasons for this failure are many. Some go back to the nature of these parties and the manner of their organization. Others are the result of external circumstances surrounding them. For the most part, these parties are weakly organized and have few members; the majority of their members come from the ranks of the educated few, distant from the common people—who in turn are too much absorbed in earning the merest livelihood to care about vague and complex national problems and issues. The common people, too, are beset by the arbitrary measures of their governments, which desire to keep the masses ignorant, removed and insulated from all political activity and organization. Furthermore, the common people are so concerned with local political conflict against local authorities and foreign agents that they have little opportunity to interest themselves in the major national problems of their fatherland.

Finally, Arab political parties and party activity are almost confined to the lands of the Fertile Crescent. Those of North Africa are taken up with the conflict against French and Spanish colonialism and local tyranny,[7] while those of Egypt and the Sudan are engrossed in combating British colonialism, absorbed in the local problems of the land, and obsessed by the myth of the Unity of the Nile Valley. As for the countries of the Arabian Peninsula, they have not yet known what political parties are, and may not for some time to come.

5. Modern Means of Communication

At the beginning of the nineteenth century, the Arab world was divided into separate lands, economically and politically disjointed and detached. Each Arab country led a life economically undeveloped and self-contained, socially backward and ingrown. Finally, however, modern means of communication which, since the beginning of the nineteenth century, were becoming common throughout Western Europe and the United States, reached the Arab world, and began to spread deep into it, slowly during the nineteenth century but with added speed during the twentieth. Railroad lines and highways linked many of its major cities, and ports equipped with all the needs of modern navigation rose where fishermen had hitherto stretched their nets. Military and civil airports were built in all Arab countries. Among the factors which hastened the introduction of these modern means of communication were the military, administrative, and commercial needs of the various powers which colonized most of its lands: the transportation of invading troops, the supply of stationed garrisons, and the steady movement of goods and products to and from newly acquired markets.

The Hejaz railroad, for example, was built by the Ottoman Sultan-Caliph 'Abd-al-Hamid II in order to enhance his reputation throughout the Moslem world and to confirm his rule of the Peninsula. This railroad, however, became one of the unifying factors, linking the Peninsula with Syria and the Fertile Crescent and making it possible for nationalists in both areas to meet, co-operate, and in the first Arab uprising strike one of the first blows for Arab unity. The Berlin-Bagdad railroad was the expression of a German dream of linking Constantinople with the Persian Gulf in order to extend German political and economic domination over the Ottoman Empire and to deal a mortal blow to British colonial bases throughout the Persian Gulf and, ultimately, in India. The First World War shattered that dream, and the German attempt succeeded only in part. The British and the French followed and accomplished what the Germans had hoped to achieve. Consequently, Iraq now enjoys the benefits of a railroad connecting its northernmost part with Basrah on the extreme south. A railroad links Syria with this line, while across the so-called Syrian Desert, foreign and local companies have opened a veritable overland highway on which motor transportation moves with ease and safety. From northern Syria a railroad extends south through Lebanon and Palestine to meet the Egyptian railroad near al-'Arish. (The overland link, rail as well as highway, between Egypt and the Asiatic parts of the Arab world has been severed since the rise of the state of Israel.) Railroad lines traverse Egypt from the north to the south as far as Wadi Halfa, where they connect with the Sudanese line.

All along the Libyan coast from the Egyptian border to Tunisia, Mussolini built paved highways which he hoped would serve the new Roman empire he dreamed of establishing. Farther west in North Africa, the French laid down a network of railroads and highways for the economic and military support of their colonial empire.

Even the Peninsula, which since its earliest habitation by man has seen only camel caravans, has been opened to and penetrated by overland motor transportation. Its most important seaport on the Persian Gulf, al-Dammam, has been recently linked by rail to al-Riyad, the Saudi Arabian capital. Plans to extend this line from al-Riyad through Medina to Jidda on the Red Sea are being seriously considered by the government.[8]

Last but not least, the advent of the airplane to the Arab skies has linked the various parts of the Arab world with a network of airlines, making it possible for the Arab to reach, in the course of a few hours, any of the far-flung points of that Arab world. It is linked, almost completely, with a network of telephones, telegraphs, and radios, as well as with a satisfactory service of ordinary and air mails.

The influence of these modern means of communication upon the economic, social, and national trends and development of the Arab world has been far-reaching. Through them, the parts of the Arab world have been physically linked together, and what is more important, all these parts have been economically and culturally linked to the outside civilized world. These modern means of communication are helping to transform Arab economy from the stage of natural production, or what might be called the economy of self-sufficiency, to that of market production, or what might be called commodity production. The farmer, for example, has been induced to produce for trading in local and foreign markets, instead of producing, as heretofore, for the satisfaction of his own needs only. Consequently, extreme and narrow provincialism has been in part transcended, contact between the countryside and the city has been made easier, and contact between city and city has been made regular and strong, with the result that each Arab country has been in practice unified.

Modern means of communication have also strengthened inter-Arab economy and encouraged cultural interaction among the different Arab lands. By enabling the Arab to travel with ease from one Arab country to another, they have given him the opportunity to emerge from his local isolation into more spacious national horizons. Likewise, they have forced the gates of the Arab world wide open to international influences, thereby enabling the Arabs to establish closer contacts with the West and to reap the benefits of what the West has in the way of ideas, reforms, and industrial progress, though they also have to suffer from what the West has brought along with it in the way of economic, military, and political colonization.

Modern means of communication have reduced the effects of natural barriers, abridged distances, and consequently made available to the Arabs, or at least to the intelligent among them, the possibilities of closer co-operation and unity.

Mention must be made also of the influence of modern means of communication upon what seems to be a trend towards the settlement of the nomadic Bedouins. Nomadism, in its very nature, conflicts with the idea of nationality and state. But the modern means of communication have made the settlement of the nomads both necessary and possible. On the one hand, the modern means of communication are competing with the Bedouins in a field which is a vital source of their livelihood—namely, transportation. On the other hand, they have enabled governments to extend their control over the desert and the remote countryside, thereby making it possible for these governments to stamp out raiding, one of the mainstays of Bedouin life. When the Bedouins are settled on the land and take up agriculture, they are gradually transformed into productive citizens, capable of comprehending what a state is and what it represents, understanding what nationalism means, and ready to labor for the achievement of its aims and aspirations.

6. Modern Economic Developments

During the Abbasid period, the Moslem world, of which the Arab world was a part, comprised one economic unit. Caravans heavily laden with various commodities and agricultural products, as well as all manner of luxury articles, traversed its different regions over well-marked and safe routes. That economic unity was to some extent the result of the then prevailing political unity of the empire, the marked progress of its industries, and the existence therein of some kinds of specialization in production, as well as the flourishing condition of its agriculture and trade. Simultaneously, that economic unity was one of the factors working for industrial progress, commercial prosperity, and political unity itself. But with the destruction of the Abbasid state under the blows of the Mongols and the Tartars, and its breakup into numerous different and conflicting states, the economic unity of the empire was likewise destroyed. The disintegration of irrigation dams, canals, and aqueducts, the decimation of the farmer class through civil wars, epidemics, and famines, and the general spread of confusion reduced agriculture to stagnation. With the deterioration of social and political conditions, industry deteriorated, and trade shrunk and became exposed to danger. The Mamelukes and later the Ottoman Turks followed, but although they were able to control the most important parts of the Arab world for several centuries, they were unable to restore its economic unity and industrial and commercial prosperity. By the beginning of the nineteenth century, the Arab countries were without exception socially backward and economically and politically disjointed.

During the century and a half which followed, changes, mostly for the better, have been brought about. The situation today is somewhat different from that which prevailed until the beginning of the nineteenth century. Economic contacts between the various Arab countries have gained in volume and intensity. The reasons for the change are many, but the most important are progress in the means of transportation, advancement of Arab agriculture from the stage of mere self-sufficiency to that of commodity production, a rise in the standard of living, especially in the cities and the growing population centers, and a marked improvement of industry and industrial skills in some Arab countries, particularly Lebanon and Syria, which have had a growing export trade to other Arab countries. Furthermore, some of the Arab countries, especially Lebanon, Syria, and Egypt, have moved far ahead of others in international trade, and have become a market place for foreign and Arab commodities, principal centers for banking and exchange operations, and depots for foreign goods which are exported to the other Arab countries.

The flourishing of economic relations among the Arab countries is one of the most important factors bringing the Arabs closer together, as it is one of the foundations upon which Arab unity, or at least genuine and effective Arab co-operation, must rise.

The strong bonds existing today between the various parts of every Arab country, which were during the nineteenth century remote from one another, are to a large extent the result of the growth of economic relations. Indeed, increasing economic contacts have made the relations between the lands of the Fertile Crescent on the whole stronger than those existing among the other Arab countries. The direct bearing of economic co-operation upon the development of Arab countries has become apparent, and the men of Arab governments and those concerned with national and economic problems have begun to take account of it.[9] When one recalls that each of the major rivers of the Arab world runs through more than one Arab land, that the blights of agriculture, such as locusts, cannot be confined to one country and cannot be fought except

43

through the active concerted effort of all, it is easy to see the necessity for co-operation among the Arabs. The same is true of the new problems arising from the building of various pipe-lines and lines of communication across Arab territories; they cannot be solved without the active co-operation of the Arab countries concerned. And finally, Arab economy today oper-ates in terms of rivalry and competition, though it is obvious that budding Arab industry cannot either be firmly established or flourish except through the co-operation of all the Arab countries in evolving a coherent and unified economic policy for the entire region. In fact this important point did not escape the notice of the framers of the Covenant of the League of Arab States. Article Two of the Covenant states:

> The purpose of the League is to draw closer the relations between member states and co-ordinate their political activities with the aim of realizing a close collaboration between them, to safeguard their indepen-dence and sovereignty, and to consider in a general way the affairs and in-terests of the Arab countries.

> It also has among its purposes a close co-operation of the member states, with due regard to the structure of each of these states and the conditions prevailing therein, in the following matters:
> (a) Economic and financial matters, including trade, customs, cur-rency, agriculture, and industry.
> (b) Communications, including railways, roads, aviation, naviga-tion, and posts and telegraphs.

The interest of Arab merchants and industrialists in eco-nomic co-operation is growing from day to day. The Chambers of Commerce of the Arab countries (representing chambers of commerce in Iraq, Syria, Lebanon, Jordan, and Egypt) have already held two conferences, the first in Alexandria during May, 1950, and the second in Beirut during January, 1951. The latter was attended by four hundred members represent-ing eighty chambers besides the delegation of the League itself. The resolutions emphasized the importance and neces-sity of strengthening the economic relations between the Arab countries by facilitating commercial exchange, studying the problem of currency unification, removing or at least lowering customs barriers, organizing a federation of Arab chambers of commerce, convening a conference of Arab chambers of commerce every nine months, and establishing a permanent secretariat for the federation, with headquarters in Beirut. The secretariat was instructed to collect such economic information and documents as concern the Arab countries and to make them available to every interested merchant, industrialist, and businessman, so that each could keep informed of developments in the Arab market, the needs of every Arab country, etc.

A glance at the many Arab banks and the numerous commercial and industrial companies, the branches of which are fast spreading into all Arab capitals and major cities, will show the extent to which Arab economy is interrelated and interacting. In spite of their growth, however, Arab economic relations are still weak and hesitant and lack firm foundations. The reasons for this weakness are many, the most important being the absence of political unity and the fact that the majority of the Arab countries are subject, in one form or another, to the domination of foreign powers, every one of which is constantly endeavoring to direct the economy of the country under its control in the direction most favorable to the interests of the foreign power. Furthermore, the fact that the Arab world is still primarily agricultural, and that production is in general geared to self-sufficiency only, has made commodity exchange between its countries weak. There is no likelihood of its flourishing until a certain amount of specialization in production exists.

Still another reason for lack of economic strength is that industry is still undeveloped in some of the Arab countries, and falls short of meeting their needs as a group. Hence the need to import finished goods in quantity. This tendency is further bolstered by the dominance of foreign powers over Arab economy and their attention to their own interests in export, import, and production. The foreign powers have consistently endeavored to retard the industrialization of Arab countries and to keep them primarily agricultural—both a market for foreign industries and a source for the raw materials needed for foreign mills.

Arab economic relations are further weakened by the meagerness of the prerequisites for heavy industries, such as raw materials, machines, technical experts, and business directors, and by the paucity of capital, the limited purchasing power of the masses, and the keen competition native industries and goods have to face from the foreign.

Because of all these factors, the economic relations between France and North Africa, for example, are stronger than those between North Africa and the other Arab countries. Similarly, the existing economic relations between Britain and the Sudan are stronger than those between the Sudan and Egypt. A similar statement may be made concerning the economic relations between Britain and Iraq, on the one hand, and between Iraq and Syria and Lebanon on the other.

Finally, the adverse effect of the existing differences in currency, customs laws, and tariff policies upon Arab economic relations should be mentioned, as well as the crippling effects of arbitrary rules and regulations restricting the free flow of capital and the movement of persons, all of which thwart the development of trade and paralyze economic progress.

The External Factors

Until the closing years of the eighteenth century, the Arab world was in a state of near stagnation, ingrown, content with its prevailing conditions, resigned to its fate, and blissfully ignorant of the events unfolding around it. Then the West descended upon the Arab world as a conqueror, bringing its culture, civilization, and science, its missionaries, moral values, and concepts, its mercantile goods and commodities, and political, economic, and military domination. This onslaught of the West, in all its forms, turned out to be the strongest challenge and the most serious danger to confront the Arab East since the period of the Crusades. The ensuing contacts —at times peaceful and at other times violent—were the first incentive to compel the Arabs to reconsider the bases upon which their spiritual, social, political, and economic order stood, to force them to think of their present, and arouse them

46

to anxiety for their future. Indeed, all the religious, national, economic, and social reform movements the Arab world has seen since the conquest of Egypt by Napoleon in 1798, regardless of the form they have assumed, have been in general natural responses on the part of the Arabs to that challenge by the West. Sometimes these movements assumed the character of assimilation with the West and of attempting to understand the spirit of its civilization and culture; at other times they were characterized by dislike, or fear, or outright hostility and opposition. Today the West is still challenging the Arabs, and the latter are still groping for the correct response to that challenge. This chapter will attempt to summarize the most important Western influences—governments, institutions, individuals, and civilization—that have awakened the Arabs, aroused their national spirit, revived their national consciousness, and brought them closer together. In this way a comprehensive summary may be had of the factors which have produced what is now seen in the Arab world of *rapprochement,* political consciousness, and the will to freedom, progress, and unity.

1. Education

Throughout the Arab countries which were under Ottoman rule, education was limited and poor. The language of instruction in the few elementary, secondary, and higher schools which the Ottoman government established in the different Arab countries was for the most part Turkish. Consequently, the benefits which the Arabs drew from these institutions of learning were very meager. Moslem religious schools, on the other hand, as well as the elementary schools *(katatib)* for boys, were, on the whole backward, and their influence upon the national awakening was almost nil.

Side by side with these government and religious institutions of learning, sectarian or parochial and foreign schools existed throughout the Arab world, except in the Peninsula. Since the Ottoman government considered every non-Moslem religious sect a separate and an independent community to be granted special concessions, including the right to have its own schools and to teach therein through its "national" language, parochial schools which employed Arabic as the language of instruction grew in those parts of the Arab world where Christian minorities lived. Initially, the majority of these sectarian or parochial schools were devoted to religious instruction. Later on, they became, under the influence of foreign secular schools, for the most part modern educational institutions. They were not, however, alone in the educational field. Beginning with the early nineteenth century, foreign schools multiplied throughout the area. Most of these foreign schools were founded and operated by missionary agencies—Russian, Italian, German, French, British, American. Of these the French Jesuit and the American Protestant institutions were the most important. These schools paid special attention to Arabic, in order to attract the native population and to achieve greater ease in the exertion of influence upon them. Furthermore, they gave modern science a prominent place in their curricula. But foreign schools did not for long remain the sole concern of missionaries. Very soon, foreign governments came to their aid throughout the Arab world, seeking thereby to extend their influence, to spread the use of their languages, and to win the populace over to their side.

Both religious and secular schools spread through all parts of the Arab world except the Peninsula, more particularly in Lebanon, Syria, and Palestine, and to a lesser extent in Iraq, Egypt, Sudan, and North Africa. The most important of these were the Jesuit University of St. Joseph and the Syrian Protestant College (later the American University) in Beirut. Foreign governments supported those schools, financially sometimes and morally at all times.[10]

The services rendered by these schools were many and important. They helped to spread the use of Arabic at a time when it was facing the threats of Turkish and illiteracy. They introduced Arab youth to modern science and acquainted them with current political, social, and intellectual movements in the West. These services were by no means limited to the ranks of Christian Arabs, but extended to vast numbers of Moslem youth who flocked to them for their introduction to modern learning. Many of their graduates, both Moslem and Christian, had far-reaching influence upon the national awakening through the books they had written, the societies they had formed, the newspapers and magazines they had published, and the many and varied services they had rendered in the field of education. These schools, too, rendered undeniable services to the Arabic language through their printing presses (mainly the American press and the Jesuit press, both in Beirut), their active interest in writing and publishing Arabic books, translating others from foreign languages, preparing a fine version of the Bible in Arabic,[11] and making other notable contributions in many fields.[12]

When the Western powers occupied the various Arab countries, they set up in every occupied country a civil administration. The need to supply the various administrations with Arab officials, clerks, and interpreters became obvious, and in turn accentuated the need for schools which would be able to equip students with modern learning and impart to them a practical knowledge of the foreign languages necessary for such officials. Perforce, when such modern schools started to appear for the service of the civil administration, it was no longer possible to arrest the process or limit its spread. The educated official could no longer neglect the education of children and let them grow up ignorant and illiterate; the illiterate man himself, on seeing what a modern education brings in the way of money, prestige, and influence, now insisted on sending his children to school; and the social reformers, who realize and value the role of the school in the reform of society and in national progress, pressed governments to build more schools, and placed such demands high in their programs. In this way modern schools multiplied throughout the Arab world.

These schools also performed another notable service. Side by side with what the West had brought to the Arab world of the fruits of its civilization, these schools were the windows

49

through which Arab youth could view Western civilization and progress. This knowledge of the civilization of Western countries, even in the face of uncivilized behavior of Occidentals in the occupied Arab countries, was among the most important factors which prompted Arab youth to demand the independence of their fatherland and strive for its reform and progress.

2. Economic Life

The influence of the West on Arab awakening and on bringing the Arabs closer together was also apparent in the field of economics. The modern means of communication which the West introduced into the Arab world (highways, railroads, telegraph, telephones, and wireless), primarily to serve its military and economic ends, became a very important factor in unifying each Arab country locally, linking its different parts closely together, and, as already mentioned, in promoting economic relations between the various Arab countries which were, until that time, sunk in provincialism. The large companies which Western businessmen, bankers, and merchants organized in the Arab world, the most important being the Iraq Petroleum Company, the Arabian-American Oil Company of Saudi Arabia, and the other petroleum companies in Kuwait and Bahrein, have greatly helped in reviving the economic life of each of these countries and in improving their material and cultural well-being. Directly and indirectly, they also brought the various Arab countries more closely together. The pipelines and roads which those companies built between Iraq, Syria, and Lebanon, and between the Saudi Arabian ports on the Persian Gulf and Jordan, Syria, and Lebanon, have firmly linked those countries together and have imposed upon both their governments and people the need for collective action and co-operation in solving at least the problems arising from those gigantic undertakings. The fantastic fortunes which those companies suddenly conjured up from the earth have forced every Arab country involved out of its indolence and have compelled it to enter into commercial and cultural relations, otherwise impossible, with the other Arab countries. The cultural, economic, and industrial revivals in Bahrein, Kuwait, Saudi Arabia, and Qatar, for example, have made it necessary for each of these countries to summon and employ hundreds of teachers, physicians, and skilled workers from Egypt, Palestine, Syria, Lebanon, and Iraq. The material advancement in these countries has strengthened the commercial relations between them and the other Arab countries, if it has not altogether created them. The Arab regions on the Persian Gulf were formerly scarcely known to the Arab public. Today they are on practically every tongue, and their news makes bold headlines in the Arabic press. They have actually become an integral part of the Arab world after remaining for centuries geographical names, known only to the educated elite.

Western powers and companies have employed thousands of Arab laborers in their communications and installations. In the nature of the case they had to train them in technical skills and operations. In so doing they have created an army of trained technicians and skilled laborers from whom the national movement benefited in general. Because of their acquired familiarity with organizational methods and their activities in labor unions, and because of the social consciousness they came to possess as a result of their new life, many of these people became very important in the national liberation movement in the Arab countries. The labor unions in Tunisia were in the vanguard of the recent struggle of their country for independence. Similarly, the Egyptian laborers manning the British installations in the Suez Canal Zone were the first to respond to their country's call when the Wafd government denounced, in 1951, the Anglo-Egyptian Treaty of 1936, leaving their stations by the thousands and all but crippling the British installation at Fayid and the other Canal bases. In Lebanon, Syria, and Iraq, labor, both union and non-union, was always in the forefront of the national struggle. In Saudi Arabia, Bahrein, Kuwait, and Qatar, the petroleum companies have transformed thousands of the native population from indolent nomads to trained workers skilled in the operation of machines. It is not unlikely that they will soon be able to apply themselves to the solution of their national problems.*

While discussing the influence of the West upon the development of Arab economic life, something must be said about the Middle East Supply Centre. Organized by the British government in 1941 with headquarters in Cairo it became in the spring of the same year an Anglo-American agency. Its purpose was to provide the inhabitants of the Middle East with the essential goods they needed in the face of wartime limitations on maritime transportation. The Centre encouraged local production of foods, aided industry, organized the distribution of rare and necessary materials, and prompted the different Middle Eastern states to co-operate in various economic enterprises. In 1944, it convened the Middle East Agricultural Development Conference at Cairo, in which all the Middle East states except Turkey exchanged information and views on the agricultural problems of their respective countries. It also convened a conference for discussing the best methods for improving census operations in the Middle East. The work of the agency came to a close with the end of the war and was succeeded by the British Middle East office. But this Office did not survive long. In spite of the limited scope of its operations and the consistent mistrust of its unlimited powers and its capacities as an instrument of foreign intervention, the Middle East Supply Centre was beneficial and had a salutary and a noticeable influence on the Arab countries where it was able to introduce ideas of organization, planning, and co-operation in economic problems.[13]

3. POLITICAL LIFE

In the field of politics, Arab contacts with the West provoked the spirit of nationalism and liberation in various forms.

---

* On October 17, 1953, about 13,000 Arab workers of the Arabian American Oil Company went out on strike, after the jailing of a group of men who claimed to represent them, demanding higher wages, extra living allowances, schools for their children and other concessions. It is of course premature to read into this event the beginning of an organized labor movement, but there can be little doubt that the jinni is already out of the bottle.

Since the beginning of the nineteenth century, Western countries, particularly Britain, France, Italy, and Germany, strove to extend their domination over the Arab world, employing every possible device to penetrate it and control its resources. Step by step they were able to occupy its various countries, subjugate its people, and exploit its wealth. Finally they took deliberate steps, not without success, to destroy Arab unity, dull Arab national feeling, and obstruct and delay as much as possible the growth of Arab national consciousness. In spite of all its adverse motives, however, this Western policy of empire engendered several developments favorable to the Arabs.

During the First World War, when the Allied Powers were locked in mortal combat with the Central Powers, the Allies sought Arab support through promises of liberation, self-determination, and independence.[14] These promises and declarations, particularly the famous Fourteen Points of Woodrow Wilson and the active propaganda which accompanied them, were instrumental in awakening Arab national consciousness, arousing the spirit of struggle, and reviving national aspirations which were buried deep beneath apathy and despair.

The period between the two World Wars became, therefore a period of open conflict between the Arabs and Britain, France, Italy, and Spain, in particular, as well as a period of concealed conflict between the Arabs and the West in general. Also, nearly every Western power tried to arouse the Arabs in every Arab country not under its domination in order to spite and embarrass its rivals, weaken their position, and extend its own spheres of influence at their expense. In the propaganda against British and French influence in the Arab world, as well as in arousing the Arabs against British and French policies of empire and kindling the spirit of nationalism among the Arabs, particularly in Egypt, Palestine, Syria, and Iraq, Nazi Germany and Fascist Italy were perhaps the most active and the most successful.

With the outbreak of the Second World War, Britain and France were locked in mortal combat with the Nazis and the

Fascists, and again turned to the Arabs for aid and support. They sought to win Arab favor, and therefore unleashed a torrent of promises and declarations pledging to fulfil Arab national aspirations and assuring the Arabs that their longing for freedom and liberation would be realized.[15] Western propaganda was very active in preaching democracy, social justice, and the right of all peoples in self-determination. The tide of national consciousness rose high among the Arab masses, their social and political horizons were enlarged, and their expectations that the end of the war would bring about the fulfilment of all these promises were greatly aroused. With the end of the War, however, Arab hopes were shattered and Allied promises again remained unfulfilled. The conflict between the Arabs and the Western powers was resumed on a much larger scale and with new methods, and on both sides with a new consciousness aroused by local and world circumstances and better trained by trials and tribulations. Furthermore, new factors arose after the War, such as the emergence of the Soviet Union as a world power (some Arabs see in it a model for what an emancipated and a liberated Arab world could accomplish in the course of a short period of time), the breaking away of China, Indonesia, India, and Pakistan from the hold of Western colonialism, the faltering of Britain and France, and the increase of American interests throughout the world, especially in the Arab East, where natural and human resources abound and where, by virtue of the strategic position of this area, the Communist world and the West face one another.

Intelligent Arabs are realizing, more and more, that their fatherland can no longer face colonialism except through concerted and co-operative action, unified in its aim and co-ordinated in its unfolding stages. They have come to realize, too, that the liberation of one Arab country is but a link in the chain of Arab liberation everywhere and a step along the path of its freedom and progress. National consciousness, therefore, has entered a new and a more enlightened stage. When the League of Arab States was formed, some of the political parties in Iraq, Syria, Egypt, and Lebanon called for the establishment of a popular league, to co-ordinate the effort of all parties throughout the Arab world, to parallel the official League, support its actions, and direct its policies. The movement faced considerable resistance and criticism from some Arab governments, and therefore did not materialize. But the idea persists, and efforts to bring it to fruition continue. A movement, enlisting a vast number of those concerned with the political and intellectual problems of the Arab world, and representing various schools of thought and ideologies, is on foot to hold a general conference of all the peoples of the Middle East, from Morocco to Iran, to discuss mutual problems, unify their goals, and co-ordinate their plans and policies towards the Western powers. Likewise, the Arab Federation in Cairo issued, on October 11, 1952, an invitation for the first congress of all Arab peoples, but it failed to convene because of conditions then prevailing in Egypt.

Although all these efforts to co-ordinate and unify Arab political endeavor have failed to materialize on the official level because of the pressure and intervention of Arab and non-Arab governments, political parties and political leaders in general have come to realize that the unification of their efforts and the co-ordination of their plans and policies are indispensable for the success of every Arab liberation movement. They are now striving to bring about Arab co-operation at the popular level.[16]

From its very inception until its tragic end, the Palestine problem has been one of the most important means in arousing the Arabs' inmost thought, driving them to think seriously of the future of their fatherland, and awakening them to the necessity of co-ordinating their plans and policies. The increasing interest of the Arabs, educated and uneducated alike, in the affairs of their own and other Arab countries, is seen in the popular demonstrations, staged whenever possible, in support of Morocco, Tunisia, and Egypt, for example, in newspaper columns and radio broadcasts, and in the literary output of writers, poets, and public speakers. These efforts stem for the most part from this new consciousness of Arab problems which was fanned to intensity by the sad fate of Palestine. Arab feeling, in any Arab country, toward their brethren in other Arab countries is no longer superficial and vague. It has become profound and real, and is growing in intensity from day to day as the suppressive measures of occupying powers become more arbitrary and violent.[17] If the right to organize in political parties and labor unions were freed from governmental restrictions, and public expression of sympathy and support were unchecked by governmental restraints and obstacles, this feeling of Arab toward Arab would grow and would be translated into a more active and positive co-operation among Arabs everywhere.

The feeling of Arab unity, the oneness of suffering under the burdens and humiliations of foreign rule and occupation, the common struggle for liberation, and the identity of fate towards which they are moving are among the most important new forces which are bringing the Arabs closer and closer together.

Divisive
Factors

VI. Dynastic Rivalries

THIS CHAPTER WILL attempt to show the extent to which the Arab kings, princes, presidents, and heads of states have been, and still are, responsible for the divisions, disagreements, and backwardness under which the Arabs labor and because of which they have not been able to match the progress of other countries and peoples. The attempt to describe these divisive factors, which might seem easy to the average run of Arab thinkers, is nevertheless difficult for any fair historian. Modern Arab history is still in the making, Arab diplomatic documents are still, for the most part, shrouded in secrecy, and whatever has been published about the deeds, plans, and intentions of their kings, princes, presidents, and heads of states has come either from the propaganda organs of followers and supporters or from the slander machines of political and personal enemies. Other available materials have often come from interested foreign powers who have rushed into print to justify their actions, camouflage their plans, and gain for their policies and proposed projects the widest possible support among the Arabs. A very small part of this body of material could be listed as authentic facts the veracity of which can be accepted by the intelligent and neutral student. Furthermore, since the Arab states are almost all subject to foreign influence, both concealed and open, it has become difficult for any historian to determine with any degree of confidence whether this action or that has emanated freely from an Arab king or president, or has been reluctantly undertaken under pressure and duress. Moreover, the problems which the Arab world confronts are neither novel nor isolated, but are rather of a chronic character and interrelated nature, engendered by numerous factors and circumstances and rendered more acute and complex by their antiquity. No attempt, however, will be made to depict the role of every Arab king or ruler in relation to the Arab problem, or assign to everyone his own particular responsibility in the present crises. Such an attempt would be long and complicated. Only those events and facts which are necessary for the explanation of the problems involved in the present study will, therefore, be cited.

Nor is it possible to determine the responsibility of the Arab heads of states in the present situation unless one defines the role every one of them plays in the government over which he presides, the extent of his influence in the direction of its affairs, and the degree to which he controls its fortunes. Under the circumstances it is sufficient to point out that the heads of the Arab states enjoy enormous powers in the conduct of the affairs of government, bordering on the absolute. The Iman in Yemen and ibn-Saud* in his kingdom rule autocratically, ostensibly deriving their powers from the *shari'ah,* but actually following the dictates of their own personal whims and wills. They consider the resources and the fortunes of the state as their own property[1] to be disbursed and disposed of according to their caprice and fancy.[2] The parts of the Peninsula, stretching along the Arabian Sea and the Persian Gulf, are governed by tribal chieftains in accordance with tribal law and practice, as well as by whatever rules and regulations were introduced by Britain for the safeguard of its vested interests and concessions. These sheikhs aspire no further than their own personal welfare, or at most no farther than their tribal boundaries, unless there be a neighboring sheikhdom or a principality against which they have some hostile design. Normally each is only interested in remaining aloof from all neighbors, "independent" within his petty state, hampered by none and nought in his autocratic rule.

In spite of the democratic form of government prevailing in them and the elected parliaments of which they boast, the countries of Egypt (even after the overthrow of the monarchy), Jordan, Iraq, and Libya are hardly different. Their heads of states enjoy no less power than that enjoyed by the autocratic kings, princes, and sheikhs of the Peninsula. Egypt, though now in form a republic, is at present governed by a military junta and admittedly expects to remain under a military dic-

---

* The death of ibn-Saud on November 9, 1953, has not yet brought a noticeable change, although high hopes are placed upon the present King Saud to modernize the state.

tatorship for at least three years.* The crowned heads of the remaining three kingdoms enjoy and exercise the right of dissolving parliament, postponing its meetings, and suspending its sessions. They too appoint cabinet ministers and dismiss them from office. Many a time the king exercises this power, dismissing a cabinet in spite of the fact that it enjoys the confidence of the majority of parliament. Rarely, therefore, has a parliament in session had the opportunity to withhold its confidence from a cabinet. Since parliamentary government in the Arab world is a farce, subject to the arbitrary control of any cabinet in office and to its blatant manipulation of elections, and since these cabinets, as already shown, are in turn subject to the arbitrary control of the heads of states, the latter enjoy and exercise control over parliaments as well. They also control the appointment of all officials within the state, major and minor, and hold in their grip most of the press, prostituting it to further their policies, to direct public opinion, to sing their praise, and to safeguard their vested interests. Furthermore, through the inordinate power they possess, they have created a new class of predatory wealthy men and feudal lords, on whom they lean to buttress their power, execute their will, and keep the public submissive and quiet. The power and influence which the presidency of the republics in Syria and Lebanon enjoy do not differ except in name from those enjoyed by the Arab kings.[3] Perhaps the only exceptions are in Tunisia and Morocco, where high-handed French rule has left the Bey and the Sultan hardly any influence outside the limits of the palace and the harem.

As a matter of fact, the system of government prevailing in all the Arab countries, no matter what form it may take and regardless of what modern or progressive paraphernalia

---

* The kaleidoscopic events in Egypt, beginning with the sudden ouster of General Najib on February 25, 1954, his sudden restoration to the Presidency on February 27, and to the Premiership on March 8, as well as the events which unfolded throughout March and early April, culminating with his removal for the second time, on April 18, from the Premiership and a declaration by the junta that the restoration of constitutional life to Egypt must be indefinitely deferred, make it difficult to predict the course of future developments. On November 14, 1954, Najib was finally relieved of the Presidency.

61

it may adopt, is tribal in its essence. Government revolves around the person of the ruler and his immediate entourage, while the majority of the people trudge along behind with their eyes closed, their personality obliterated, their will denied, and their goal unknown. If what has already been stated concerning the power and influence of rulers in the Arab world is true, and it is indeed true and clearly visible to anyone who has the most cursory familiarity with the internal affairs of the area, the responsibility of those rulers in perpetuating Arab differences, disagreements, divisions, and backwardness is indeed great; and it is aggravated by the fact that the Arab world has been for centuries behind the times, stagnant, and for the most part subjugated and held back by foreign domination. Were it not for the support and approval of those native rulers, foreign rule alone could not have succeeded in perpetuating the nomadism under which many of the Arabs live, the ignorance which spreads its darkness upon their homes, the disease which threatens their bodies with decay, and the poverty which ravishes their personal dignity and limits their human horizons, although they live in the midst of plenty, surrounded by fertile lands where fresh waters abound and petroleum gushes out from the earth. Furthermore, those time-honored and ancient causes of backwardness could not have remained unconquered and unsolved in the twentieth century if, in the service of their people, those native rulers had been honest in their intentions, serious in their efforts, and single in their purpose. The deep-rooted causes of backwardness have consistently reduced the majority of the people to insignificance and have rendered them, so far as their contribution to the fatherland is concerned, negligible and incapable of thinking of its well-being, either locally or nationally. Finally, they have given rulers freedom to conduct themselves according to their personal desires, unrestrained by either civic or national interest. Herein lies, perhaps, one of the most important divisive factors in the Arab world, and the one which has done most to bring about the deterioration of the Arab front in international affairs. For any idea concerning Arab unity or genuine and effective Arab *rapprochement* and co-operation cannot become a reality unless it becomes first a doctrine, accepted by the majority of an Arab public which has been freed from ignorance and poverty and which strives for that unity intelligently and deliberately and forces its rulers to do the same.

In addition to having been instrumental in keeping their people away from active participation in local Arab politics, these ruling dynasties have been a persistent factor in weakening the Arab front and in dividing the Arabs among themselves, particularly through their violent feuds, which have produced continued bitterness, rancor, and deep-seated enmities among the various royal families, and have carried these sentiments of ill will and hate to the rank and file of their subjects. Consequently, inter-Arab relations have been characterized by suspicion, wariness, and even bad faith. Such serious charges call for evidence, or at least samples of it. Here are a few examples of these dynastic feuds and rivalries:

Since the beginning of the twentieth century, the balance of power in the Peninsula has been greatly and repeatedly disturbed. Ottoman influence over the Desert receded, and its effective control was confined to the lands of the Fertile Crescent, wherein the Ottoman Turks centered their power and bolstered their rule, linking the area to their aging Empire administratively, economically, and culturally. The Arab countries stretching along the Persian Gulf and the Arabian Sea were brought within the orbit of British protection through treaties and agreements which Britain concluded with their sheikhs and princes. The remaining parts of the Peninsula were divided among five ruling dynasties, every one of which was constantly trying to enlarge its territory and extend its sway at the expense of its neighbors. These struggles continued from the turn of the century until the middle of its thirties. The Iman Yahya succeeded in unifying the Zaidis and establishing his power over Yemen. Both 'Abd-al-Hamid II and the Young Turks after him failed in their repeated attempts to subdue the country completely. After several rebellions led by him, the Imam Yahya forced his entry into San'a' in 1911, and established his control over the mountainous parts of the interior. The Turks recognized his authority, and were not able to retain more than a nominal influence limited to the coastal regions. In Asir, al-Sayyid Mohammed 'Ali al-Idrisi declared his rebellion against the Ottomans, and succeeded, with Italian help, in breaking away effectively from the power of the Ottomans just before the First World War. In Nejd, the Sultan 'Abd-al-'Aziz ibn-Saud was able, with the help of the Emir of Kuwait, to regain Riyad from the Rashid family in 1902, and to extend his control over the rest of the area. Seizing the opportunity of Ottoman weakness as well as the Empire's involvement in the Balkan War, in 1913 he occupied with the agreement of the British Indian Government, al-Ahsa' on the Persian Gulf. The region was then subject to the Ottoman wali of Bagdad. Northern Nejd was under the control of the Rashid family, with Ha'il as the capital of their principality. Only the Hejaz, along the Red Sea, was an Ottoman *wilayah* (province), administered by an Ottoman governor with the help of the Sharif of Mecca, whose most important function was the custody of the Kaaba and the supervision of the affairs of the Pilgrimage. After their revolution in 1908, the Young Turks selected for this position Husayn ibn-'Ali ibn-'Awn. The selection was made contrary to the wishes of 'Abd-al-Hamid. The new Sharif was very ambitious and resourceful. He was also in constant touch with the budding nationalist movement in the Arab world, particularly the Fertile Crescent. From the day he assumed his duties, he applied himself to the task of establishing his effective control over the Hejaz, spreading his influence over its scattered tribes, and promoting his leadership among those engaged in Arab national problems. Gradually his powers overshadowed those of the Ottoman wali and he became the veritable secular and spiritual ruler of the Hejaz, the Holy Land of Islam.

When, in 1914, the First World War broke out, the British started to look for allies among the princes of the Peninsula. The Imam of Yemen, perhaps because of Italian influence, declared his neutrality. Al-Idrisi decided in favor of the British and entered into an alliance with them in 1915. Ibn-Saud followed suit, while his inveterate enemy, ibn-al-Rashid, joined the Turks, who had been giving him aid against the Wahhabi chieftain. For a while the Sharif of Mecca remained aloof, but finally cast his lot with the British and was destined to become their foremost Arab ally and the leader of the Great Arab Revolt. For the British were also looking for an Arab leader who would lead the entire Peninsula against the Turks. Some disagreement arose among the British political experts as to whom they should pick and support for this role. The Indian government favored ibn-Saud and wished to see him pushed to the front and supported. At the same time, T. E. Lawrence and his associates in Cairo favored the support of Husayn, the ambitious Sharif of Mecca. Their advice prevailed, and negotiations between the Sharif and the British representatives in Egypt were set in motion. After some delay an agreement was reached whereby Britain would be ready to recognize and support Arab independence throughout the Peninsula and the Fertile Crescent, excepting those regions which were of particular interest to France and over which the French aspired to extend their control, the regions already under British protection, and the regions with the princes of which Britain was bound by an alliance. The negotiations were embodied in eight letters known as the McMahon Correspondence.[4] On June 10, 1916, the Sharif declared the Arab revolt against the Turk. His troops took part in the War along with the Allied forces. The Turks were driven from the Hejaz and finally the Allies occupied Syria. A number of the other Arabian princes welcomed the Revolt, and at a meeting held at Kuwait and attended by ibn-Saud, the Emir of Kuwait, the Sheikh of al-Muhammarah, and more than a hundred and fifty other persons, including some of the powerful sheikhs of smaller tribes, declared their support of the movement. While his sons were waging a successful war against the Turks, Husayn, the Sharif, was active in consolidating his grip over the Hejaz. On October 29, 1916, the same year, he promoted the Meccan sharifs to declare him "King of the Arabs," and on November 2, he formally accepted their homage. This action of Husayn was received by the major Allied Powers with a great deal of surprise and consternation, since it was in effect an encroachment upon the prerogatives of some of the other princes of the Peninsula, who were ready to accept Husayn as a peer, and might have accepted him as a leader, but who had no desire to acknowledge him as "King of the Arabs." Britain, France, and Italy, therefore, recognized him only as King of the Hejaz. He persisted, however, in calling himself, in all his dealings with his own subjects and with his neighbors, "King of the Arabs" or "King of the Arab Countries," against explicit Allied advice to relinquish the use of such a title, because of its disturbing influence upon the other princes of the Peninsula, and because of the doubts it raised in their minds concerning his intentions.

King Husayn, particularly after he had declared his revolt against the Turks, was wont to regard himself as the standard-bearer of the Arab cause and the sole champion of Arab national aspirations. As the high-sounding title which he had bestowed upon himself or had the sharifs of Mecca bestow upon him would indicate, he had an ambition to become head of the Greater Arab State. Immediately after the abolition of the Caliphate by the Kemalist Turks, in March, 1924, he accepted a hastily improvised proclamation of himself as Caliph, a fact which corroborates the suspicion that he had always entertained such an ambition. At the same time, 'Abd-al-'Aziz ibn-Saud was grooming himself for the overlordship of Arabia, deeming himself the supreme head of the Wahhabi movement which he hoped would one day envelop the entire Peninsula. If he had declared his support of Husayn's revolt, he had done so only because of his dislike of the Turks and his loyalty to the British, but he was by no means prepared to acknowledge the supremacy of Husayn's leadership. Had the latter succeeded in composing his differences with ibn-Saud he would in all probability have averted the catastrophe. But in spite of the ability and farsightedness he had shown in the preparation of the Revolt, he revealed himself wanting in the attributes of real statesmanship when it came to building up a new order in the Peninsula. His first mistake had been to assume that his sponsorship of the Revolt entitled him to political authority over his neighbors. Both the Idrisi and ibn-Saud had welcomed his alliance with Great Britain and his rupture with Turkey, and they had readily agreed that he should lead the Arab insurgence; but they had no thought of placing themselves in vassalage to him or of abating their claims to full sovereignty in their own dominions. This is why they resented Husayn's assumption of the title of King of the Arab Countries, with its implication of all-embracing sovereignty. In the case of ibn-Saud, the position was made worse by the fact that he was the head of the vigorous Wahhabi revival, with missionary activities reaching out beyond the confines of Nejd and into territories regarded by Husayn as owing allegiance to him.[5] The clash between these two Arab princes, each of whom was striving to extend his control over the entire Peninsula, seemed inevitable. Disagreement over the borders added to the strain. Throughout the War, Husayn tried to compose these differences, but did not, and could not, succeed. His highhanded methods and his condescending and even discourteous attitude towards the Wahhabi head ruled out any possibility of success, and accentuated ibn-Saud's suspicions of his good intentions, particularly since Husayn's position was weaker, his armed forces being smaller and his international relations more confused and unsettled.[6]

The first serious clash between the two occurred on May 19, 1919, near Tarabah, on the eastern borders of the Hejaz, where ibn-Saud's Wahhabi forces all but annihilated a Hejaz army led by Husayn's son, the Emir Abdullah. The Wahhabi victory was decisive, and had it not been for the timely intervention of Britain, which compelled her ally, ibn-Saud, to stop (both he and Husayn were receiving an annual grant), his forces could have pushed on to the Hejaz unopposed. The memory of this battle rankled in the mind of Husayn and his son. He therefore would not heed the advice of Britain and of his

Arab friends and well-wishers to resolve his troubles with ibn-Saud and conclude peace with him, but remained adamant and continued to hatch his intrigues in secret against his Wahhabi foe. He therefore concluded an alliance with ibn-Saud's bitter enemy, ibn-al-Rashid, and with other hostile sheikhs on the outskirts of the Nejd. He also tried to conclude a similar alliance with the Imam of Yemen. On the other hand, ibn-Saud's victory over Husayn freed him to turn his attention to the Rashid family, who had been weakened by the collapse of the Ottoman empire and the British occupation of Iraq, and against whom he had unsettled accounts, particularly after they had routed him at the battle of Jurab in 1915. In the autumn of 1921, therefore, he attacked Ha'il and succeeded in bringing the rule of the Rashids to an end and in extending his control over all their domains, annexing the entire Shammar to Nejd and thereby bringing his northern boundaries to those of Iraq.

After destroying the Rashidid power, there was nothing left for ibn-Saud except to settle his accounts with Husayn. After the War, Husayn's troubles had multiplied, and his position had become shaky. Britain had not fulfilled the promises it had made to him, but divided between France and herself the country which was to have made his dream of the Greater Arab Empire come true. Because of his uncompromising position on Palestine, Britain no longer supported him in his struggle against his Wahhabi foe. Likewise, his continued disagreement with ibn-Saud contributed to the weakening of his position vis-a-vis Britain. Instead of peacefully resolving his differences with ibn-Saud, in order to free himself to deal with Britain, he further strained his relations with ibn-Saud. Moreover he failed to establish good government in the Hejaz, and mistreated the pilgrims who annually flocked to the Holy Cities of Islam. His conduct toward his neighbors led to one crisis after another, particularly with Egypt and the Idrisi. The situation was aggravated further and his position among the Arabs and the Moslems was weakened still more when he succumbed to the wishes of his son Abdullah, then the Emir of Transjordan, and accepted the title of Caliph, following the abolition of the Caliphate by the Kemalist Turks and their exile of the last Ottoman incumbent, 'Abd-al-Majid II. Husayn's acceptance of this august anachronism gave ibn-Saud the opportunity to fight him as an innovator who had broken away from the catholic consent of the community of the faithful, and to depict Husayn before Moslem opinion as a selfish opportunist, bent upon achieving his personal ambitions of setting himself ruler over the Arabs and the Moslems at the expense of Islam and the believers in Islam. The Wahhabis then attacked al-Ta'if during the last week of August, 1925, destroying the city and killing the majority of its inhabitants. Terror spread throughout the remainder of the country, and the inhabitants of Mecca, hoping to escape a similar fate, requested Husayn to abdicate the throne. He stepped down in favor of his son 'Ali and left the Hejaz for Akaba. The British forced him from Akaba (ostensibly to avoid an attack on it by ibn-Saud, who was claiming it as part of his territory), and allowed him to seek refuge in Cyprus. 'Ali, the new king, was unable to withstand the onslaught of the Wahhabi hordes. He therefore surrendered (January, 1925) and left the Hejaz for the court of his brother in Bagdad, where he lived in exile. On January 8, 1926, 'Abd-al-'Aziz ibn-Saud was proclaimed King over the Hejaz.

Relations between the Imam of Yemen and al-Idrisi of Asir were also strained, riddled with mistrust, suspicion, fear, and hate. Since the evacuation of Yemen by the Turks immediately after the First World War, the Imam had become its absolute ruler. He also aspired to extend his boundaries to include the territories which he and his followers claimed to be the historical boundaries of Yemen. This would have meant the seizure of vast portions of Asir. He likewise regarded Idrisi as a weak and boastful lackey of the British. After the surrender of the Turkish garrison in Yemen following the end of the War, the British had occupied al-Hudaidah, the main port of Yemen throughout the Turkish period. On December 31, 1921, the British finally evacuated the city, and permitted Idrisi to occupy it and to annex it to his domains, thereby denying to the Yemen access to a natural and essential port used by it for centuries. This was perhaps the most important cause of the increased tension between the two potentates. After the death, in the early part of 1923, of the Sayyid Mohammed, the head of the Idrisid dynasty, conditions in Asir became unsettled, and civil war broke out between his successor and other members of the family. This seemed a good opportunity for the Imam to seize. He therefore proceeded to occupy the southern region of Asir as well as a large portion of the coast, including al-Hudaidah. The Idrisid ruler appealed to ibn-Saud for help, but the latter refused to intervene. When, however, he discovered that the Imam intended in his struggle with the Idrisids, to annex the southern regions of Asir in their entirety to Yemen, he changed his mind and concluded with the Idrisid ruler a treaty[7] whereby Asir placed itself under the protection of ibn-Saud. The Idrisids, however, were unable to resolve their trouble with Yemen, but found themselves compelled either to submit to the Imam or merge with the Saudis. They chose the lesser of the two evils, and, therefore, a new agreement with ibn-Saud was concluded in 1930, under which Asir officially became a Saudi protectorate. To all practical purposes it became a part of the Kingdom of Saudi Arabia, thereby bringing ibn-Saud and the Imam face to face in the struggle for the Peninsula.

Ibn-Saud proclaimed Asir a protectorate of his in order to arrest the expansion of the Imam, who had already regained al-Hudaidah, the plains of Tihamah, and a mountainous and a coastal region which the Idrisids had occupied. After negotiations which dragged on for three years in an attempt to settle border disputes over some of the outlying regions, war broke out between the two countries, and the victory of the Wahhabis was both quick and decisive. The war ended with the Treaty of al-Ta'if, concluded on May 20, 1934, in which the Imam recognized his original borders and relinquished all demands for the annexation of any new regions to his territory.

These bloody struggles between the princes of the Peninsula ended with the destruction of the Emirate of the Rashidids in Shammar, the Kingdom of the Hashimites in the Hejaz, and the Sultanate of the Idrisids in Asir. Ibn-Saud emerged the absolute lord of the Peninsula, while the Imam shut himself up in Yemen, taking only remote interest in Arab affairs. These struggles between the Arab princes were among the hardest blows to befall the Arab movement. They weakened the efforts of Arab patriots who were struggling for the liberation of their countries in North Africa, Egypt, and the Fertile Crescent. While Iraqis, Egyptians, and Syrians were measuring swords with British and French occupation forces superior to them in organization, money, and equipment, the princes of the Peninsula were overexerting themselves in the search for a span of territory which one could extort from the other, oblivious of the agonies of their fellow Arabs in the occupied Arab countries and of the hardships inflicted upon them by the invaders. They gave them no help, and hardly even thought of them.[8] Likewise, these feuds weakened the position of the Arab governments vis-a-vis the Western powers after the First World War. For had King Husayn been in agreement with the Saudi Sultan, his position vis-a-vis Britain would have been stronger, and Britain might not have been able to leave him in the lurch and abandon him so completely. Similarly the fate of Syria, Iraq, and even Palestine might have been better.

While the princes of the Peninsula were singing of Arab unity, Arab federation, and Arab co-operation, they were busy plotting to destroy one another. On the day Ameen Rihani called upon King Husayn to bid him farewell, the King, holding his beard, said, "I do not seek or desire it [i. e., Arab leadership], no, I do not seek or desire it. Let the princes of the Arabs agree on it and I shall retire. Let them agree on supporting Arab unity and I shall, if they so desire, withdraw, subscribing to whatever they agree on, regardless of whether I shall be merely a follower or the one followed. I say, thou brilliant Professor, merely a follower or the one followed."[9] Nevertheless he always insisted on calling himself King of the Arabs and never would accept any other title, nor could he

71

bring himself to the approval of any transaction with another Arab prince who did not acknowledge him as such. Rihani further states:

Arab unity was the topic of our discussion during many a meeting. But when the day of my departure drew near, the Sultan ['Abd-al-'Aziz] spoke at length on the subject. I, therefore, recorded the gist of his remarks that evening and submitted the result to the Sultan the following evening for his approval or correction. I submit to the reader the statement before and after:

Sultan 'Abd-al-'Aziz' Opinion on Arab Unity

"1. He seeks Arab unity and would help anyone who would sincerely seek its fulfilment. He would attend a meeting held for that purpose, and would accept Arab leadership and homage as king over all Arab lands because he believed he was fit and qualified for the position and capable of strengthening it.

"2. If the Arabs should select as head any other than himself, he would accept their selection and would not be dissuaded from his belief in Arab unity, but would continue to serve the Arab cause to the best of his abilities.

"3. At any rate, he is a man of peace within his domains. He has no desire to attack anyone, and would not allow any one to attack him."

That same evening, I jotted down the gist of the conversation, as recorded above, and submitted it to the Sultan for his scrutiny and approval. He read the statement, article by article, and then reached his pen and struck the second, saying, "You have misunderstood what we meant in this second article. We would not make any statement to be quoted by the Professor and then fail to stand by it. But this cannot be." Pointing to the second article, he resumed, "We know ourselves, and would not accept the leadership of any other."

The reader would recall the words of King Husayn at the moment I bid him farewell. "I do not seek or desire it [i.e., Arab Leadership] . . . and I shall work for its fulfillment [i.e., Arab unity] . . . regardless of whether I shall be merely a follower or the one followed." The reader would likewise recall how King Husayn refused to sign the two treaties, one with the Imam and the other with the Idrisi, because neither would acknowledge him leader of all the Arabs and would not hail him King of the Arabs.[10]

The struggle between King Husayn and ibn-Saud ended in that tragic way, but the enmity between them did not end. The Hashimites in Iraq and Jordan have not forgotten that ibn-Saud expelled them from their country, seized their dominion, and humiliated them before themselves and before the world. Nor had ibn-Saud himself forgotten that he had disinherited the fathers of the ruling monarch of Iraq and Jordan, driven them out of their homes, and sent them into exile. He had, therefore, up to the time of his death, continued to fear them and to suspect all their actions and all their plans.[11] Inter-Arab policies have since that day become riddled with misgiving, suspicion, and bad faith. These have been reflected and continue to be evident in the ceaseless disagreements among the members of the League of Arab States, in the Palestine problem, the Greater Syria Plan, the various plans for the unification of Iraq and Jordan, and in other major Arab issues.

The rivalries which have flared up around the Greater Syria Plan, in particular, would explain the nature of the relations which have existed and still exist among Arab rulers, and the extent to which these relations have influenced inter-Arab co-operation and Arab policies on other major Arab issues in general. To understand the Greater Syria Plan, it is necessary to examine the foundations upon which it was based and the motives which have governed it during the last few years.

These Arab countries which were known as Syria (al-Diyar al-Shamiyyah, or Bilad al-Sham, or al-Barr al-Shami), and which are now known as Geographic Syria, comprising the present Republic of Syria, the Republic of Lebanon, as well as what was, up to 1948, Transjordan and Palestine, form one geographical and economic unit. During the Ottoman period all had similar administrations with the exception of the Lebanon, which after the events of 1860 was separated from the other parts and given a special autonomous status and a local administration headed by a Christian governor who was aided by an administrative council representing the population.

The modern Arab nationalist movement first appeared in Syria. Political societies and parties became active throughout the area, as well as in Constantinople and some European capitals. They asserted the right of the Arabs to national sovereignty and independence, and demanded liberation from Ottoman rule. In this movement, Syria sacrificed a good deal and suffered from Ottoman domination. Therefore when Husayn launched his revolt against the Ottoman Turks, Syrians were quick to lend their aid to his movement and hastened to the support of his son Faysal when the latter entered Damascus triumphantly on October 2, 1918. The national movement in Syria sprang up to uphold the independence of the country. Of the parties which took active part in the national movement, mention should be made of the Hizb al-Ittihad al-Suri (the Syrian Federal Party), founded by a number of prominent Syrians residing in Egypt. Its demands may be summarized as follows: To constitute Geographic Syria, from the Taurus Mountains in the north, the Khabur River and the Euphrates in the east, the Arabian Desert and Mada'in Salih in the south, and the Red Sea, Akaba, Rafah, and the Mediterranean in the west, into a sovereign state enjoying complete independence guaranteed by the League of Nations. Another party, al-Hizb al-Watani al-Suri (the National Syrian Party), appeared in Damascus, championing not only the demands put forth by the Syrian Federal Party but also the promotion of the national, cultural, and economic relations between the various parts of the Arab world. As for the form of government, the National Syrian Party demanded a constitutional monarchy, with Faysal ibn-Husayn as king, and a government responsible to a parliament representing the people. The plebiscite conducted by the American King-Crane Commission in 1919 revealed the overwhelming majority of the Syrians as favoring Syrian unity, complete independence, the establishment of representative government with Faysal as king, and decentralization of administration. All rejected the Zionists' claims in Palestine.

Britain and France, however, had other plans. Arab demands in Syria for liberation, independence, and unity were ignored, and the two powers were determined to carry out the terms of the well-known Sykes-Picot Agreement. As his father's representative, therefore, Faysal proceeded to Versailles

74

in order to submit the Arab case before the Peace Conference. His demands, however, failed to receive any sympathetic hearing. The great Allied powers were busy apportioning the conquered territories among the victors. After several unsuccessful attempts to reach some understanding with Britain and France, he was compelled, under British pressure, to meet with Clemenceau, on November 27, 1919, and to accept the bases of a temporary agreement between the Arabs and France. These enjoined the Arab Kingdom in the interior of Syria to accept the French occupation of the Lebanon and the other coastal regions of Syria up to Alexandretta in the north. The Bekaa Valley was to be a neutral area separating the French from the Arab administration. The agreement also decreed that the Arab Kingdom should henceforth depend on France for any aid (financial, technical, economic, educational, etc.) it might need. Reaction in Syria was both immediate and violent. Syrians disapproved of the Faysal-Clemenceau agreement, feeling that Faysal had betrayed them and sold the country out to the French. The instructions he had received from his father and the unanimous Arab rejection of any partition of Syria, or the imposition of any form of foreign trusteeship or mandate, made the Syrians feel Faysal had surrendered matters he had no right to surrender. On his return to Damascus on January 14, 1920, he soon discovered that his popularity had waned and that people were receiving him with aversion wherever he went.

A constitutional assembly representing all the Syrian provinces was elected.[12] It held its first meeting on March 8, 1920. The resolutions it passed included the following:

The General Syrian Congress, fully representing the entire Syrian nation with its three regions—the interior, the coastal, and the southern (Palestine)—resolves and publicly announces: The complete independence of Syria within its geographic limits (including Palestine) and the establishment of a civil representative government. . . . We have chosen His Highness the Emir Faysal . . . to be a constitutional king over Syria. . . . The provinces will enjoy a decentralized administration. In the administration of the Lebanon, within its pre-war boundaries, the aspirations of the Lebanese will be fully recognized, provided it remains removed from any foreign influence. . . . Whereas the Arab Revolt was declared in order to accomplish the liberation of the Arabs from Turkish rule, and whereas the foundations upon which the independence of Syria rests are the same as those upon which the independence of Iraq also rests, and whereas the two countries are linked together by linguistic, historical, economic, natural, and racial bonds, making each indispensable to the other, we therefore demand the complete independence of the Iraq, with the condition that there be a political and an economic federal union between the two sister countries.[13]

In a statement before the General Syrian Congress, made on March 27, 1920, the Syrian Cabinet declared its support and adherence to the resolution. Similarly, the second Syrian Cabinet, in a statement before the National Congress on May 20, 1920, reiterated that support.

The Supreme Allied Council met at San Remo, and on April 25, 1920, reached a decision whereby the entire Arab rectangle, from the Mediterranean to the Persian borders, was to be put under a "mandate." Geographic Syria was to be divided into three separate parts: Palestine, Lebanon, and Syria. Syria and Lebanon were placed under the French mandate, while Palestine shared the fate of Iraq, both having been placed under the British mandate, but with two separate administrations. Immediately after the San Remo decisions were made public, France began its preparations to occupy the Syrian interior. On July 14, 1920, therefore, General Gouraud dispatched his well-known ultimatum to King Faysal, in which he demanded that Syria unconditionally accept the French mandate, rescind the law for compulsory military conscription, and reduce the size of the Arab army. Faysal decided to accept all these conditions without question, but by so doing he provoked the dismay and the anger of his aides and exposed himself to the indignation of the populace. A message he received from Lord Curzon, advising him to avoid collision with the French at any cost, encouraged him to go ahead with the enforcement of his decision. But the National Congress, backed by the Syrian people, rejected the ultimatum and decided to resist to the end. On July 19, therefore, it issued a proclamation in which it declared that ". . . should the present government violate its formal statement and fail to carry out its obligations towards the country, and should it decide to sign a document contrary to the decisions of the Congress, the Congress would consider it illegal." The government, however, began to implement the conditions of the ultimatum on the evening of the same day. On the following morning a royal decree suspended the meetings of the Congress for a period of two months, and the French troops began their march against Damascus. The people's resentment was lashed into fury and revolt. The King replied with violence, and his police killed more than a hundred persons in the streets of Damascus. Maysalun followed—the battle which, fought between the Syrians and the advancing French army on July 22, at a place a few miles west of Damascus, decided the fate of Syria for the next quarter of a century.

The first thing the French did in Damascus was to invite Faysal to leave. On July 28, 1920, he departed with his close friends, having lost not only his throne but also the great popularity he had enjoyed with the Syrians, who had truly loved him. The period of the Hashimites in Syria ended only to usher in a period of blood, sweat, and tears for the Syrians in their struggle against the French mandate for the next two decades.

During those twenty years the French established their rule over Syria and Lebanon with violence. They dismembered the country and proceeded to direct its economy, administration, and culture in such a way as to insure and promote their interests and to entrench their influence. The British carved out the southern part of Syria to create Transjordan, over which they enthroned Abdullah ibn-Husayn as prince, and exploited their mandate over Palestine to enable Zionism to grow and expand. Syrians and Palestinians were left, all alone, to combat the British and French mandates and Zionist inroads, while the Princes of the Peninsula were preoccupied with their own feuds and King Faysal was busy consolidating his throne in Iraq. As to the Emir Abdullah, the British mandate left him no opportunity for any national endeavor save to dream his dreams of empire and to sing the glories of the Great Arab Revolt, his heart festering with rancor against all the Arab princes without exception, not even his own brother Faysal, whom he persistently accused of usurping the throne of Iraq on the grounds that a group of Iraqi youth in Damascus had declared Abdullah himself King of Iraq at the time Faysal was declared King of Syria by the Syrians.

With the collapse of France at the beginning of the Second World War, Britain decided upon the occupation of Syria and Lebanon in collaboration with the Free French Forces. At that time, both Britain and the Free French promised independence to both countries. As a result of popular Syrian and Lebanese efforts, all but unique international circumstances, and a genuine desire on the part of President Franklin D. Roosevelt to make of Syria and Lebanon a model of what small nations should expect after Allied liberation, that promise was actually fulfilled, and both countries were declared independent republics.

It was at this juncture that Abdullah entered upon the scene and launched his propaganda for the Greater Syria Plan. Actually, the Plan is divided into two parts. The first calls for the establishment of a unified state in Geographic Syria (comprising Syria, Lebanon, Palestine, and Transjordan), sovereign and independent. The form of government proposed is a constitutional monarchy. Certain regions in Palestine and the Lebanon (i.e., Mount Lebanon, which formed the old administrative unit under the Ottomans) would have a special administration. Upon the formal establishment of this unified Syrian state, steps would be taken to organize an Arab federal union of the unified Syrian state and of Iraq (the area often now called the Fertile Crescent) which would co-ordinate their policies of defense, education, economics, and politics. The plan would also leave the door open for the other Arab states to join the federal union. The second plan calls for the establishment of a federal Syrian state within an Arab federation. Regardless of whether the future state should be unified or federated, its head would be the Emir Abdullah. He would be invited to head the Syrian state because of the following considerations:

1. His established legal rights in the principality of Transjordan, which is an important part of Greater Syria.
2. His past and present effective aid to the Allied cause, which, in the present [Second World] war included action in the Syrian theatre.
3. His being the foremost heir of his father, King Husayn, in guarding Arab rights in general and Syrian rights in particular.
4. The British government's promise to him, in 1921, through its [present] Prime Minister, Mr. Winston Churchill, to head the Syrian state, and the disappearance, through the fall of France and the loss of its legal representation of the League of Nations, of the obstacles which have hitherto stood in the way of the fulfilment of that promise, particularly that Britain has now gained freedom of action throughout all Syrian territories.
5. Syrian preference and desire for a constitutional monarchy, in the event the country is either unified or federated.[14]

Abdullah carried on propaganda for his plan and induced his supporters to promote it, but the war conditions and the lack of stability in Syria and Lebanon gave him no opportunity for any extensive effort. With the end of the War, however, his propaganda for Greater Syria became very active again, especially after the termination of the mandate in Transjordan, which the opponents of the plan used as an argument against it. Abdullah rested his claims for Greater Syria on the same bases on which the Syrian Congress had rested its demands for a unified Syrian state, but without taking into consideration the changes which two decades had brought into the scene. Slowly but surely, Zionism had penetrated into Palestine; the British mandate had entrenched itself in Transjordan, its influence reaching every corner; conditions in Syria and Lebanon had changed, the people having made noticeable progress materially and culturally and the national movement itself having developed greatly since the time of the Arab Revolt. Furthermore, the attitude of the people towards the Hashimites had changed completely, just as their attitude towards the monarchical form of government had changed. In both Syria and Lebanon there grew up a ruling class whose concern was to maintain its sole control over government, and a citizenry in maintaining its independence and preserving its democratic institutions and republican form of government.

The Greater Syria Plan stirred up throughout the Arab world a violent argument which preoccupied the Arabs and the Arab governments for a considerable period of time. Governments and political parties alike attacked it from every angle, and for several years the press opened its columns to news of it. In spite of its Hashimite exterior, to some it was nothing but a British plan, using Abdullah, Britain's friend, executor of her policies, and guardian of her interests in the Arab world, to drive out the vestiges of French influence in the area and to displace it by her own, and to preoccupy the Arabs in order to divert them from their struggle for liberation and to distract them from any constructive effort in Palestine, which the British were preparing to hand over completely to the Zionists. To others it was a Zionist plan, designed to extend Zionism beyond the borders of Palestine. Almost all its political opponents attributed it to Abdullah's personal ambitions, which titillated him with the possibility of sitting on the throne of Syria and Lebanon, of which he dreamt for many years, and for which he was prepared to pay any price, not excluding Arab unity and independence.

As to the Arab governments, their attitude toward the Plan was not uniform. Iraq supported it because it would extend and enlarge Hashimite power. Syria and Lebanon rejected it and would have nothing to do with it. Egypt viewed it with disfavor, while Saudi Arabia attacked it most violently. On August 31, 1947, the Saudi Arabian government issued the following statement:

> A statement, attributed to His Majesty, King Abdullah ibn-al-Husayn, and dated Amman, Ramadan 17, 1366, has come to the attention of the Saudi Arabian government. In it he called upon the Syrians, in unmistakable terms, to convene a meeting for changing the Syrian Constitution. He further stated that he intended to see to it that the change was made. He followed that [threat] with a letter which he addressed, on Ramadan 28, to the President of the Syrian Republic.

While regretting the fissure thus caused in the ranks of the Arab states, the Saudi Arabian government considers this action of King Abdullah to be contrary to all international laws, as it is also contrary to the Covenant of the United Nations Organization. The Saudi Arabian government also considers that action in clear contradiction of the letter, spirit, purposes, and aims of the Covenant of the League of Arab States, violating its Eighth Article in a most flagrant manner.

The Saudi Arabian government regrets the existence of any disagreement in the ranks of the Arab States, particularly at this very critical period through which many of the Arab countries are going.

[These countries] had hoped that all the resources of the Arab States should have been devoted to the salvation of the Arab fatherland rather than for the shattering of its unity and agreement.

While declaring its regret for the appearance of this new fissure, it declares, in no mistaken terms, that it considers this action [of King Abdullah] a brazen attack upon Syria and upon its republican constitution, which was adopted and approved by the nation and recognized by the other governments of the world, thus giving Syria the international position worthy of it.

At the time King Abdullah advocates the destruction of this youthful Arab state, the Saudi Arabian government, while condemning this attack, declares its support to Syrian independence and hopes that the other members of the League of Arab States will abide with [the terms of] the treaties and agreements which they have entered.[15]

As to the League of Arab States, it delivered itself from the embarrassment in a graceful manner by issuing a statement at once satisfactory to the Syrians and the Lebanese, relieving the Arab states from the necessity of opposing the Plan, and not hurting the feelings of King Abdullah himself.[16]

The fact of the matter is that this Plan, which King Abdullah continued to advocate up to the very day on which he was assassinated, had done the Arab cause grave injury, dividing the Arabs where it had hoped to unite them. It preoccupied the Arab governments and the Arabs, diverting their attention from their basic problems. It revived enmities which were better buried, strengthened the spirit of provincialism in every country which came into its scope, frightened Syria and drove it into the lap of ibn-Saud, spread terror among the advocates of Lebanese separatism, increasing their suspicions and apprehensions of any movement towards Arab co-operation and *rapprochement,* and accentuated the division of the Arab states into two rival camps: the Amman-Bagdad axis and the Riyad-Damascus-Cairo axis.

The problem of monarchical union did not end with the death of King Abdullah. No sooner had the Jordanian throne become vacant than a new plan calling for the unification of Jordan and Iraq under the crown of Faysal II, or, as an alternative, the unification of Jordan and Syria (of course under the Hashimites) was put forward. The Hashimites of Iraq welcomed the new plan, if actually they did not inspire it. The ruling class in Jordan, which was created by King Abdullah and the British mandate, opposed it and did its best to thwart its fulfilment. Syria and Lebanon saw in the new plan a Hashimite maneuver to encircle them and force upon them the Greater Syria Plan. The press, therefore, unleashed its attack upon it, and Shishakli* denounced it with the following statement: "If Jordan is to unite with any Arab country it had better unite with Syria. Jordan was a part of Syria, carved out [by the foreigner]. That part should be restored to the mother country." The Egyptian and the Saudi Arabian governments opposed it, while the opposition press in Iraq saw in it a British plan designed to place the burden of the covert British mandate in Jordan on the Iraqis, and to consolidate British control over Iraq.

In spite of seemingly cordial relations among the Arab kings and rulers, and in spite of their constant protestations in favor of Arab union, the deep-seated enmity among ruling

---

* Adib al-Shishakli, at the time strong man of Syria and its virtual dictator. He had been active behind the scenes in every military coup d'etat in Syria until he staged his own on December 19, 1949. He continued to rule behind a façade of constitutionality until the fall of 1951, when he ousted the President of the Republic and assumed direct control himself. In June, 1953, he issued a new constitution; in July, he assumed the combined office of President and Prime Minister; and in October, he was elected President. On February 25, 1954, he was overthrown and forced to flee the country by still another coup d'etat, and the President whom he had ousted in 1951 was restored to office.

Arab dynasties and the bitter rivalries among them have been among the most important divisive factors, wrenching Arab countries far apart, diverting the Arabs from their basic problems, and weakening them before those forces which threaten them from within and from without. The League of Arab States has become, in the eyes of intelligent Arabs a laughing stock and a farce, especially since its failure to co-ordinate the efforts of the Arab states and to harmonize their policies so as to face and solve the major Arab problems, the most important of which is that of Palestine. The founding of the League promised to be the fulfilment of a dream which has long stirred the imagination of the Arab nationalists, and the realization of a hope which has long swelled in their hearts. Its failure was, therefore, a great disappointment. Yet the League itself has not failed. The idea upon which it was based was neither wrong nor fantastic. But the architects who raised it on bitter rivalries, festering rancors, and deep-seated enmities failed and caused the faith of many Arabs in the idea itself to waver. At a press conference in Bagdad, Dr. Mohammed Fadil al-Jamali,* Iraq's Foreign Minister and head of the Iraqi delegation to the League, made the following statement: "One of the weaknesses of the League of Arab States was its slow pace, resulting from the presence of opposing groupings and incompatible personalities, of which none of the responsible persons in government throughout the Arab world was unaware, ever since the formation of the League. . . ."[17] Dr. Jamali also pointed out, at the same conference, "that the disappearance of some of the incompatible Arab rulers would help in bringing about greater co-operation [within the League], since the crisis of the League was basically the result of disagreements between the heads of the various [Arab] governments. The death of King Abdullah, the disappearance of Faruq, and the removal of 'Azzam, all these have created a new atmosphere. . . ." Palestine itself might have not been lost and its inhabitants might have not been driven into a homeless diaspora if the hatreds and the enmities of the ruling

---

*Recently Iraq's Prime Minister; he resigned on April 21, 1954.

83

Arab dynasties had not thwarted Arab co-operation and undermined their position in the Palestine war. Had these dynasties been able to agree at the first appearance of Zionist danger in the early twenties, they might have succeeded in solving the Palestine problem long before Zionism became a serious threat.

The story would not be complete without making at least a cursory mention (because official and reliable documents are not yet accessible or available) of the disagreements which arose among the Arab troops fighting in Palestine, and which led to their failure to co-operate in the field, the defeat of the Egyptian forces at Falujah, the handing over to Ramlah and Lydda[18] to Israel without consulting either the Palestinians or the other Arab governments, the creation of what was known as the All Palestine Government (Hukumat 'Umum Filastin) under the aegis of Egypt, and the seizure of the remnants of Palestine by King Abdullah. In the thick of the Palestine war, the ruling Arab dynasties were busy wrangling over the division of loot—the Palestine loot.

VII. The Foreign Powers

THE HISTORY OF Western colonialism in the Arab world is well known. Ever since the West had set out on its policy of empire and expansion at the beginning of the seventeenth century, and, more particularly, since the so-called Industrial Revolution beginning in the latter part of the eighteenth century, the Arab world has been a coveted prize and a cornerstone in the edifice of empire. From the early part of the nineteenth century on, the Arab countries extending along the coasts of the Arabian Sea and the Persian Gulf were one by one brought under British control. When the twentieth century began, all these lands were under British protection. In 1882, Britain occupied Egypt, and in 1898, with Egyptian soldiers, occupied the Sudan. France occupied Algeria in 1830, Tunisia in 1881, and Morocco in 1912; and in the same year Spain also seized the northern parts of the country. In 1912, Italy too entered the race for empire and occupied the coastal regions of Tripolitania, completing the occupation of the interior of that country in the third decade of the twentieth century. During the First World War, Britain and France joined in the occupation of Iraq and Syria, including the Lebanon, Palestine, and Transjordan.

The motives for this occupation are likewise well known. They are the motives for any colonialism. These are basically the advantages to be had from the strategic position of the land, the exploitation of its natural and human resources, the development of the country as a source of raw materials and as a market for manufactured goods, and as a place for the investment of excess capital. Colonial powers never lacked occasions for the justification of their policy of empire and territorial expansion. These include punitive expeditions against rebellious sheikhs whose pirates terrorized shipping across the seas, or whose tribal brigands threatened commercial caravans across overland trade routes; the protection of foreign nationals or religious minorities; forestalling occupation by a rival who was preparing to seize the area and thus threatening the interests and influence of the colonial power therein and endangering its acquired rights and privileges in the neighboring countries; the liberation of the native population from an oppressor and improving their living conditions and sharing with them the benefits of Western civilization; and the realization of the Christian ideals of human brotherhood, co-operation, and equality throughout the world.

An attempt will be made to determine the extent to which Western colonialism has been, and is now, responsible for destroying the unity of the Arab world by isolating one Arab country from another, weakening the forces of liberation and unity within it, retarding its economic development, and obstructing its educational and cultural progress; and to show the methods which Western powers have used and still use in promoting and consolidating their influence in the Arab countries. It must be pointed out, however, that if no mention is made of the many services and benefits which the Western powers have rendered to the Arab world, this is true not because of any unawareness of these services and benefits or because of any desire to deny them, but because this investigation is not concerned with all the activities of the Western powers in the Arab world, but rather with one aspect of these activities only: namely, the influence of the Western powers in dividing the Arab world, driving each Arab country away from the others, and slowing down their progress.

Western powers have pursued a policy of dismemberment in the Arab countries they have occupied, have prevented the union of one with another, and have obstructed every effort of *rapprochement* among them. This is natural; it stems from the very essence of the policy of empire. A united country is difficult to prevail over and to control. Once overpowered by another through the latter's military or economic superiority, the problem of keeping it subjugated will arise. The conquering power, concerned primarily with the safeguarding of its interests and the maintenance of its control, proceeds to dismember the conquered territory and to divide its inhabitants into hostile groups and opposing factions. This time-honored policy has hampered the development of the modern Arab movement from the first.

At the beginning of the nineteenth century, Mohammed 'Ali Pasha sought to establish a unified Arab empire. Britain, however, opposed the idea, and did not stop until it was jettisoned. Britain feared that the rise of a strong Arab power which could displace the weak Ottomans in that part of the world might endanger its commercial interests and threaten the lifelines of its far-flung empire. In a letter addressed to the British diplomatic agent in Naples, dated March 21, 1833, Palmerston wrote: "His [Mehemed-'Ali's] real design is to establish an Arabian kingdom including all the countries in which Arabic is the language. There might be no harm in such a thing in itself; but as it would imply the dismemberment of Turkey, we could not agree to it. Besides, Turkey is as good an occupier of the road to India as an active Arabian sovereign would be."[1]

This was Britain's policy toward Arab unity before it spread its control over the Arab world. As soon as Britain was able to subjugate the various Arab countries, she proceeded to dismember them and to sow the seeds of dissension among their ruling princes. In fact this is how she was able to maintain her domination over the Arab coastlands from Aden to Kuwait. These outstretched coasts were the habitat of various Arab tribes, for the most part nomadic. By following a policy of "divide and rule" among their princes and sheikhs, supporting one family aspiring to power against the ruling family, and intervening in local politics whenever a ruler was about to be chosen, Britain was able to extend her rule over the entire area. At times she bore heavily upon the sheikhs, resorting to threats and intimidation; at other times she indulgently cajoled them with gifts, subsidies, and titles. She promised every prince or sheikh that she would safeguard his "independence," and would oppose and turn back any aggression to which he might be exposed by hostile Arab princes from within, or by ambitious foreign powers from without. Finally, Britain's policy was to bind every one of these sheikhs or princes with a treaty which placed his territories under her protection. Actually these "protectorates" were identical with outright occupation. The treaties stipulated among other things that the prince or sheikh should not conclude any alliance with any of his neighbors or with any other foreign power, and that he should not sell or rent or relinquish any part of his territory without first consulting the British resident, or governor. Furthermore, in their dealings with the tribes, the British not infrequently followed an inhuman policy of discord. They would arouse one tribe against the other to insure themselves against the possibility of tribal unity against them.* In this way, Britain was

---

*"The wisdom, or otherwise, of *Divide and Rule* has often been discussed. Limited as were his military resources, and the reinforcements he asked to punish the Lahej being vetoed or delayed, Haines felt he had no option but to pit one tribe against another, and he advocated 'setting other hostile tribes against the marauders without calling in British Bayonets.' Money is the sinews of war, and Haines believed in its charm and potency. . . . It is sad to note the wobbling policy of the Government of Bombay, who in 1846, with seven years' experience of Aden, and after having proscribed most of the measures advocated by Haines, were ready to approve of dissen-

able to create in the Aden Protectorate (Hadramaut) more than thirty independent sultanates, emirates, and sheikhdoms, although the entire population was scarcely over half a million. Likewise, Britain was able to erect within the narrow coastland stretching from Oman to Qatar, with an area not exceeding 6,000 square miles and a population of about 80,000, six independent sheikhdoms. Within each of these the ruling sheikh is as jealous of his independence, influence, and authority as he is of his own life.

In the words of General Maude's* well-known proclamation to the people of Bagdad, Britain and France entered Syria, during the First World War, as "liberators, not conquerors." Indeed, the Arabs participated in the War as allies, fighting side by side with the British and the French, and expected that the pledges made to the Sharif Husayn for independence and aid in the establishment of an independent and unified Arab state would be fulfilled. But the British and the French were bent upon carrying out the terms of the Sykes-Picot Agreement and the Balfour Declaration. In its original form the Sykes-Picot Agreement was not easy to implement. Britain was anxious to get the rich Mosul oil fields and to have a free hand in Palestine. France, on the other hand, was determined to occupy the Syrian interior without competition from any source. At the San Remo Conference in 1920, an agreement was reached whereby Britain would occupy Iraq, including Mosul, while France would occupy Syria and the Lebanon. Britain would not insist upon the independence of the Syrian interior, and France would receive a share in the Mosul oil. Palestine and the remainder of Syria would go to Britain. The dividing line between the two occupations was fixed south of Deraa.

Under the Ottomans, the southern part of Syria formed the Mutasarrifiyyah of Karak. During the time of the short-lived

---

sions between the Abdali and the Fadli, for 'though loss of life is to be regretted, still the occurrence, it is hoped, will prove beneficial to British interests at Aden by widening the breach between the respective tribes' " (Harold F. Jacob, *Kings of Arabia,* London, 1923, p. 45).

*Sir F. Stanley Maude, Lieut-General, commanding British forces in Iraq. The proclamation was issued on March 19, 1917.

Arab state in Syria, it formed the Mutasarrifiyyah of Salt. British policy, however, called for the creation out of this small, barren, and certainly non-viable region, lacking all the prerequisites of statehood, the principality of Transjordan with Abdullah ibn-al-Husayn on its throne. The principality was placed under British mandate, and, administratively under the jurisdiction of the British High Commissioner in Palestine. The greater part of the budget, of course, was borne by Britain. The *raison d'être,* if any, was British desire to benefit from the strategic position of the region, which controls all the adjacent Arab countries.[2]

Britain used its mandate over Palestine to facilitate Zionist immigration by the thousands. With British help and encouragement, the Zionists acquired the fertile areas of Palestine and established in them their farm colonies and industries. Arab opposition to Zionism and constant Arab insurrections and revolts against the mandatory power for the liberation of the Holy Land and the attainment of its independence were put down by the British in the harshest manner. Systematically disarming the Arab population, it helped the Zionists to build up their power and indulgently overlooked the terroristic activities of their extremist elements, even when these activities were perpetrated against its own officials and soldiers in the area.[3] Official American pressure on behalf of the Zionists gave Britain a convenient excuse to throw the whole responsibility into the lap of the newly organized United Nations General Assembly. On April 2, 1947, therefore, it requested the calling of a special session of the Assembly to consider the problem, and announced its intention to terminate the mandate. The outcome was inevitable. On November 29, 1947, the United Nations voted to recommend the Partition of Palestine. Even before the date set for the withdrawal of its troops—May 15, 1948—Britain withdrew and left the country in a state of chaos, having done all it could throughout its twenty-eight-year mandate to insure the fulfilment of the Zionist dream. The story after the British evacuation is well known. With United States financial and moral support,* Israel became a reality, and about one million Palestinian Arabs became homeless refugees. Except for colonialism, the Arabs have never faced a greater and a more dangerous threat than that of Israel. For the first time since the period of the Crusades, when petty states arose in Palestine and in the coastal regions of Syria, a hostile and foreign state has arisen in the midst of the Arab world, destroying its ethnic and geographic unity and threatening it with the specter of total political and economic domination. Furthermore, Israel constitutes a potential ally to those Western powers holding interests in the Arab world, and with Israel's help they can readily threaten any liberation movement forming in any adjacent Arab country.[4]

In Syria the map was drawn by France in accordance with its own policy of empire. The Lebanon had for long been the stronghold of French influence in the eastern Levant. The majority of the Lebanese were Maronite Christians and traditional friends of France, as were several other Uniate† groups who considered France their traditional protector. Syria was, on the other hand, predominantly Moslem and the center of the Arab national movement. Consequently France pursued a different policy with each. It enlarged the Lebanon at the expense of Syria, annexing to it the Syrian regions immediately adjacent to it on the north, east, and south, the coastal cities of Tripoli, Beirut, Tyre, and Sidon, the interior city of Baalbak, and the fertile Bekaa Valley. As to Syria itself, the French proceeded to tear it apart, partitioning it into four

---

* One might even say indirect American military support, because the Truman administration consistently refused to take any serious steps to stop the flow of military aid to Israel from the United States itself. It is true that this aid was not governmental and official, but the government which forced the Armistice upon the Arabs would not raise a finger to stop some of its own citizens from smuggling military planes and arms to the Zionists in Palestine. The United States' role in the creation of Israel is well known. Without United States intervention in the United Nations, the Partition of Palestine would probably never have been approved by that body. Only through continued United States aid, official and private, has Israel been able to survive thus far.

† Christians of the Eastern rite acknowledging the Pope's primacy, and agreeing with the Latin Church in matters of faith, but differing from it in liturgy and discipline.

independent states. These were the government of Latakia (al-Ladhiqiyyah) consisting of the coastal region between the Grand Liban† and the Senjak of Alexandretta (al-Iskanda-run), with Latakia as capital; the Druze Mountain (Jebel al-Duruz), consisting of the mountainous region between Damascus and Transjordan, with al-Suwayda as capital; Syria, consisting of the remainder of the territory under French mandate, with Damascus as capital; and the Senjak of Alexandretta, which enjoyed a special administration despite its official link with Syria.

The aim of France in dividing Syria into these four separate states was to stimulate the growth of a regional as opposed to a national outlook, strengthen sectarian cleavages, and undermine the unifying efforts of the Arab movement. French policy also aimed at weakening the Arabic language and falsifying Arab history. It imposed the teaching of French in all official schools and its use, alongside Arabic, in law courts and government bureaus. Through these acts France hoped to obstruct Arab progress towards unity and independence.[5]

French policies and actions went farther than that dismemberment of Syria and the division of Syrians into conflicting groups and hostile factions. Part of Syria was carved out and delivered to Turkey without either the consultation or the consent of the Syrians. In a way, the fate of Alexandretta was similar to that of Palestine. Just as Britain handed over Palestine to the Zionists, France handed Alexandretta to the Turks. The Senjak, including the city of Antioch, has an area of 1,930 square miles and a population of 228,000. Of these, 85,000 are Turks, while the rest are Arabs (23,000 Sunnite Moslems, 62,000 Shiite Moslems known as Alawites, and 49,000 Christians of various sects). In 1923, at the Lausanne Conference, Turkey had officially recognized the end of its sovereignty over its former Arab provinces, including Alexandretta. France, however, separated the Senjak administratively from Syria in

---

† The Grand Liban is the Greater Lebanon proclaimed by General Gouraud on August 31, 1921, consisting of the Lebanon together with the regions on its immediate north, east, and south, annexed to it by the French. It is now known as the Republic of Lebanon, and will henceforth be referred to as Lebanon.

order to destroy Syrian unity and to encourage racial and religious cleavages. As the national movement became stronger and negotiations with the French for the complete independence of Syria were begun in 1936, Turkey feared that the termination of the French mandate would restore the Senjak to Syria. With Turkish instigation and support, unrest flared up in Antioch. To win Turkish support and favor, especially in the troubled international scene prior to the Second World War, France was anxious to accede to Turkish demands. She therefore took the initiative in bringing the matter before the Council of the League of Nations. A commission was dispatched to investigate the situation in Alexandretta, and the League decided to grant the Senjak autonomy under its own supervision. The Council therefore issued a law regulating the government of the region. The legislative power would be assumed by an assembly chosen by a college of electors selected by popular vote. The executive powers would be vested in a French commissioner with power to veto, aided by a police force of 15,000 Frenchmen. Special guarantees for the Turkish population of the Senjak were pledged, and Turkish was declared an official language along with Arabic. The new arrangements pleased neither the Arabs nor the Turks. France then proceeded to deal directly with Turkey, paying no attention to either the League or to the Arabs. In August, 1938, it reached an agreement with Turkey whereby Alexandretta was declared a Franco-Turkish condominium, and a Turkish force equal in size to the French marched in to share the responsibility of policing the area, pending a general election to determine its future status. In spite of feverish Turkish activity to insure favorable returns, the elections gave Turkey only twenty-two of the forty seats in the Assembly. On September 2, 1938, the Assembly met at Antioch, and promptly declared the Senjak autonomous under the name of the Republic of Hatay. It also elected a Turkish Speaker and a Turkish Prime Minister, and adopted a flag almost identical with that of Turkey. Henceforth the Turks proceeded to Turkify the area. Turkish was declared the sole official language and the medium of instruction in all schools. Arab officials, whether Moslem or Christian, were removed. In June, 1939, as the storm of the Second World War was gathering, France voluntarily relinquished the area to Turkey. Through French machination and duplicity, Syria lost part of its homeland to its former oppressor.[6]

Besides destroying the geographic unity of the Arab world, the colonial powers endeavored to destroy its social, economic, and spiritual unity and tried their best to delay its progress. In Iraq, the British encouraged religious and racial conflicts. They moved very slowly in the field of education, since their sole purpose was the training of the clerks and interpreters they needed in the civil administration of government. In the field of national economy, they controlled the country's most important resources and facilities: petroleum, railroads, and the port of Basrah. Their monopolistic companies controlled the country's most important products, such as dates, wheat, and grain. Finally, the British have opposed and still oppose the industrialization of the country. "In fact in the mandated territories there was among the foreign observers and government circles a decidedly negative attitude towards the tendencies to industrialization. . . . The Western Powers could not reconcile themselves to the emergence of national, i.e. independent, industries which would tend to restrict the market for their own export products."[7] British obstruction of native industry took many forms. At times the local market was flooded with foreign goods in order to crowd out native products and strangle the budding native industries. At other times the importation of necessary equipment was hampered and native plans for enlargement and growth were held back, or normal industrial operations were interrupted by technical supervisors who were strategically placed in every governmental bureau in any way connected with industry.

The government under the British mandate invigorated Iraqi feudalism and strengthened its foundations. It gave the feudal lords freedom to acquire vast lands and to exploit the labor of thousands of peasants. Likewise it empowered them to extend their control over the government in order to insure through them the continuation of its influence and the realization of its aims. Feudalism has been the ally of occupying governments in the Arab world. In Iraq, the bulk of the land is government domain. Those in authority, therefore, can readily help any one they may favor to acquire whatever land he desires.

During the First World War, the British forces found themselves in need of the tribal sheikhs' aid against the Turks, by taking part in the war effort, or at least by remaining neutral and withholding their assistance from the Turks and desisting from disturbing public order throughout the land. During both the occupation and the mandate periods, the British gave the arable lands of Iraq to reward loyalty, compensate support, and win friends, or took them away to punish opponents and chastise enemies. The landholdings of those who were loyal to British rule expanded at the expense of the government domain, while the holdings of those who took part in the revolution of 1920 shrank.

British authorities also consolidated the privileges of the feudal sheikhs and increased their power, particularly through the enactment of laws and regulations, the most serious of which was the 1922 Code for Civil and Criminal Cases among the Tribes.[8] The situation was rendered more serious by the fact that the majority of the population is tribal. By making a segment of the population subject to one code and the other to a second, differing in its basic concepts and application, Iraqi unity has been undermined. By bestowing upon the tribal population special privileges not enjoyed by the urban, and by preserving tribal customs and practices incompatible with the norms of civilized societies and with the spirit of good citizenship, the processes of urbanization and progress have been impeded. By increasing the power of the sheikhs, who in most cases form the arbitration councils and are usually constrained in their judgments by their tribal values and institutions, an obstacle has been placed in the way of establishing public security in the land, and the dispensation of equal justice before the law to all citizens has been impeded. Perhaps this is what the authors of the law planned, since their main concern has been to keep the country divided, the tribal sheikhs in constant strife, and the people ignorant, holding fast to their tribal traditions and primitive customs, in order to facilitate the authors' control over the country. This and similar reactionary laws and regulations, such as the law governing the rights and duties of farm owners[9] and the law introducing a new type of tenure, called the *Lizmah*,[10] have written into the law special privileges of the feudal lords. The invasion of parliamentary life and close contacts with the government have increased their power and made them almost absolute in their farms and villages, where officials do their bidding either for fear of retribution or for hope of reward.

The net result has been that the majority of the population of Iraq have remained tribal and primitive, enslaved by their sheikhs and chieftains, illiterate, ridden by disease, malnutrition, and even hunger, and exist with a generally depressed standard of living. For the most part they are nomadic Bedouins who have no concept of nationalism, Arab or otherwise, and who have no knowledge of anything called the Arab nation to which they could be loyal or of an Arab cause which they could serve. A nomad's horizon does not reach beyond his own clan or hair-tent village; his only loyalty is to his own tribe. National feeling and tribal loyalty are different and incompatible. When it is also recalled that the democratic system of government which the mandatory power introduced into Iraq was only nominal, and that it was a distorted structure built on the shaky foundations of feudalism and tribalism, the reason for the failure of the majority of the people in Iraq to participate in the political life of the country, and in the Arab national effort in general, becomes clear. Whenever feudalism is strengthened and its influence entrenched, the inevitable result is the impediment of the growth of national consciousness and the removal of the public from active participation in government. These results in turn give both the ruling dynasties and the foreign powers—neither of which is eager for either Arab unity or co-operation—free scope to do whatever they wish with the fortunes of the Arab world.

This policy was not limited to Iraq, but was also implemented, with minor modifications, in Transjordan, Egypt, and the Sudan. Perhaps the Sudan offers the best example. In 1881 the religious leader Mohammed Ahmad al-Mahdi revolted against the Egyptian government, defeated its garrisons, and with lightning speed proceeded to extend his control over the country. In 1883, a year after Britain had occupied Egypt, she found herself unable to check the movement, and was prepared to relinquish the Sudan entirely to the Mahdi. She therefore requested the Egyptian government to withdraw its troops from the Sudan. In 1885 the Mahdi died, and was succeeded by Abdullah al-Ta'ayishi. Eleven years later, in 1896, Britain decided upon the reconquest of the country on behalf of Egypt. An Egyptian expeditionary force under the leadership of Lord Kitchener was ordered to undertake the campaign. Two years later it succeeded in destroying the Mahdi's empire. The following year, 1899, the British and the Egyptian government reached an agreement whereby both would share in the government of the Sudan as a condominium. Actually, however, Britain controlled the administration and thus governed the country alone. When in 1924 the Sirdar was assassinated by Egyptian nationalists, Britain seized the opportunity to rid itself of the remnants of the Egyptian garrison in the Sudan, and ended the Egyptian administration of the country, leaving Egypt a purely nominal partner. Britain then proceeded to isolate the country from Egypt to such an extent that it became easier for an Egyptian to travel to any other part of the world than to the Sudan. Economically and culturally, too, the Sudan was isolated from Egypt. In the Sudan itself, Britain cut off the three southern provinces, where the majority of the inhabitants are non-Arab tribes, and attempted to prevent the infiltration of Islam and of Arabic into the area, at the same time giving Christian missionaries freedom to proselyte and build schools, hoping thereby to render the separation of these provinces from the rest of the Sudan inevitable. For Arabic has always been the natural ally of Islam. Britain then moved to exploit the deep religious sentiment of the Sudanese in order to promote her interests and to consolidate her rule. The policy was carried out in the following manner:

Even before the rise of the Mahdi, the Sudan boasted of numerous Sufi religious orders. In fact it is hard to find a Sudanese Moslem not affiliated with one order or another. As it is natural to expect, differences and rivalries exist among these orders. This is so, in particular, in the case of the Mahdists, followers of the Mahdi, and the Khatmists, followers of the Khatmiyyah order headed by Sayyid 'Ali al-Mirghani. When, after the defeat of the Mahdi's power, Britain tried to stamp out Mahdism itself from the land and to destroy its military and spiritual vestiges, she brought along from Egypt the then head of the Khatmiyyah, al-Sayyid 'Ali, who had fled with his father, al-Sayyid Mohammed 'Uthman al-Mirghani, after the Mahdi rebellion. His religious influence, supported by British official influence, had a far-reaching effect in bringing about stability and in crushing the power of the Mahdiyyah order. Britain made al-Mirghani the prime leader of the Sudan, bestowed upon him a British knighthood, granted him vast areas of land, and increased the sources of his wealth. At the same time it pursued the Mahdi's immediate family, of whom none survived except an infant son born after the death of his father. But the spirit of Mahdism and its ideas, though quiescent, were far from extinct, and the many followers of the order remained loyal to its teachings. During the First World War, Britain had to keep the Sudan pacified. She therefore restored the Great Mahdi's only male survivor, al-Sayyid al-Siddiq 'Abd-al-Rahman ibn-al-Mahdi al-Kabir, to favor, bestowed upon him a knighthood, fortified his influence, and granted him extensive fertile lands in the Jazirah. Both al-Mirghani and 'Abd-al-Rahman al-Mahdi became instruments with which Britain accomplished the final subjugation of the Sudan, as well as the division of the Sudanese

97

into two contending parties. For Sudanese political parties revolve around these two personalities, religious institutions center on them, and youth organizations and clubs are controlled by them and by their supporters.

After the Second World War the nationalist movement in Egypt and the Sudan became active, and the idea of unity between the two countries was being pushed by an ever-increasing number of Sudanese. The Mahdi 'Abd-al-Rahman then emerged, with British blessings, as the leader of the Sudan. His followers, who formed a majority in the constitutional society which the British convened to lay down a constitution for the Sudan, demanded independence and complete separation from Egypt. Britain thus hoped to be able to confront Egypt with the Mahdi and to assume the role of a champion of Sudanese aspirations for self-determination.[11]

In devising and carrying out policies for subjugating the Arabs, keeping them disunited, and suppressing every sentiment of freedom among them, the French surpassed their British allies and rivals. The key to their policy is to isolate their North African empire from the Arab world as completely as possible, and to transform it gradually to a region where the language, culture, and spirit are French. In Tunisia and Morocco, the temporary protectorates were reconstituted as permanent occupations. Government bureaus are filled by French officials who control and direct the foreign and internal affairs of the two countries in accordance with the demands of French interests, without reference to what Tunisians and Moroccans may desire or think. Algeria, on the other hand, was declared part of metropolitan France as early as 1848, eighteen years after its occupation. To maintain the isolation of these regions from the rest of the Arab world, every national uprising, rebellion, and movement against French colonial rule has been suppressed in the harshest manner. Furthermore, France declared a relentless war of annihilation against the components of Arabism in the area. French displaced Arabic as the official language in governmental affairs and as the medium of instruction in all government schools. Arabic was consequently confined within the limits of the few religious institutions and private schools operated by the Moslems. Its share of time in the official curriculum followed by government schools was reduced to a minimum, and careless methods of instruction imparted it to the students disfigured and deformed. It was also made to stand the rivalry of the vernacular, which the French considered an independent language, and which they encouraged and promoted in order to sap the vitality of literary Arabic. The schools in Algeria do not offer instruction in either Arab or Moslem history, but Algerian students are required to study French history in the closest detail. Whenever Arab history is offered, it is for the purpose of disparaging it, and to show that North Africans are not Arabs and that those bonds which link them to the Arabs and the Moslems are not worthy to be retained by educated and cultured people. As to Arabic newspapers and periodicals, their number is small and their circulation is limited; at the same time they have to face the competition of local and foreign French papers and magazines with which the reading public is flooded. Stringent government regulations have also restricted the entry of Arabic printed material into any of the North African countries under French domination.

The North African economy was also given a French direction to such an extent that 75 per cent of Algerian foreign trade and 50 per cent of Moroccan trade are with metropolitan France. On the other hand, trade relations with the other Arab countries were restricted, and the region as a whole was isolated from personal Arab contacts from outside. Perhaps more serious than all this was France's encouragement of European, particularly French, immigration to North Africa, and her facilitating for immigrants the acquisition of agricultural lands. Thousands of such immigrants, called *colons,* flocked to the region and occupied the best lands. They became as far as France was concerned, the legal native settlers, while they threw their weight with French colonial policies, supporting French rule and indefinitely prolonging French occupation. Of the 3,230,000 inhabitants of Tunisia, 250,000 are

Europeans. This quarter of a million *colons* hold over 30 per cent of the arable land, good for wheat, grain, fruit trees, and olives. In other words, they own 1,239,000 hectares out of a total of 3,766,000 hectares. Because they employ modern means of farming, these *colons* produce over 50 per cent of the total annual agricultural output of the country. The population of Algeria is estimated at over 8,000,000, of whom about a million are Europeans. The extent of the arable lands exploited by 25,000 of these *colons* is 2,700,000 hectares, while the entire arable property owned by Algerians (532,000 land-owners) is 7,673,000 hectares. In other words, a group of European *colons* in Algeria who form less than a twentieth of all Algerian landowners, own lands equalling in area almost two-fifths of all the landholdings of the native Algerian population.[12] In Morocco there are 400,000 Europeans. The *colons* among them own 4,000 modern farms, occupying 7 per cent of all arable lands in Morocco, and producing 15 per cent of the grain harvest and 80 per cent of the citrus crop of the entire country.[13]

The 1,600,000 Europeans in North Africa, of whom the majority are French, control the region. They have a veritable monopoly over the central administration; local legislative and municipal councils are at their service; the fertile arable lands are their property; industry and commerce are at their disposal; and schools built and supported from the central treasury are set aside for the education of their children. The Arab share in this partnership has as yet failed to show anything but greater poverty and continued ignorance. These are evident to the visitor to the native quarters in the North African cities.

The Arab features of North Africa are further endangered by the *colons*, who because of the factors already enumerated, are unable to hold their own and to perpetuate their economic and political privileges unless the region continues under French rule and unless it is still further isolated from the other Arab countries. For this reason they continue to oppose any liberation movement designed to separate the region from France, and continue to dictate French North African policy.

General Augustin Guillaume, former French Resident in North Africa, states that "though the Europeans are only 5 per cent of the population, they provide the majority of the administrators and the technicians, and the taxes on their economic activities provide half of the state income; the size of their economic stake in the country makes it impossible for them to accept the position of a political minority."[14]

General Guillaume further states that "by geography, by the ethnic origins of the major part of its population, North Africa was an integral part of Europe when the latter was developing in its Mediterranean cradle. . . . Only its Moslem religion, the tribal organization of its rural population and the theocratic form of its government link it to the East."[15] In spite of what may seem falsification, this statement contains a germ of truth. The natives of North Africa are Moslems who hold fast to Islam. Their devotion to their faith is rendered more tenacious, and even fanatical, because of the ever increasing French pressure against them and against the tenets of their Arab and Moslem existence. Consequently Islam has become an instrument of protest and resistance against the French and the battle cry in all native struggles against the invader. These two bonds, Islam and the Arabic language, are the strongest ties which bind North Africa to the Arab world. Actually they are the two factors which have enabled the region to remain Arab and Moslem under French rule and domination. Should the French succeed in destroying, or at least weakening, Islam, just as they have succeeded in weakening the Arabic language, North Africans would become docile and submissive, and would no longer resist the invader's plans for their Frankification. This seems to be the cornerstone of French policy in North Africa. This is why the French have bent all their efforts upon fighting Islam and weakening its foundations, especially among the Berbers. To that end the French are attempting to revive Berber languages and dialects and to restore Berber traditions and customs by writing them into law or giving them the strength and character of law . To that end, too, the French have prompted Christian mission-

101

aries to infiltrate the area and have aided them in their efforts at proselyting. At the same time the spread of Islam and its strongest ally, Arabic, have been checked by means of the well-known law which goes under the name of al-Zahir al-Barbari (the Berber law).

In Spanish Morocco and Tangier, Spanish policy and actions have not been different from those of the French in North Africa except perhaps in details. The aim, spirit, and harshness are similar. The current effort of Franco's Spain to effect a *rapprochement* with the Arab world should be considered a temporary and expedient measure, designed to divert Arab attention from its acts of aggression in the Riff and to win Arab support in international affairs.

The Second World War brought about the liberation of Libya from Italian domination (since 1912, and more particularly since the advent of Fascism, Italy had followed a policy of annihilation against the native population), only to bring it under a British influence, overt and covert, similar to that already seen in Iraq, Egypt, the Sudan, and especially Jordan. Finally, the so-called "cold war" brought to the entire North African littoral the United States of America with its vast air bases and military port installations, making the United States appear, perforce, as a new factor in consolidating Western power and control, in buttressing colonial domination internally and externally, and raising still another obstacle against Arab liberation.

As a matter of fact, the "cold war" has almost literally placed the Arab world, so to speak, between two millstones: the United States and Russia. These two states have emerged from the Second World War as the two leading powers of the world, with a determining influence on the policies and actions of all nations. If for no other reason, they are a current factor in Arab affairs.

In the case of the United States, however, it is the failure to develop a long-range and an independent Arab policy of her own, not necessarily parallel to those of her allies or subject to local political pressures, which is at the root of the trouble. Until the Second World War, American interests in the Arab world, which were almost exclusively religious, educational, and humanitarian, were insufficient to necessitate a policy. Now the Arab world has claimed the interest of the United States as a global center of gravity, both in times of peace and in times of war. The importance of Arab petroleum production to free world economy, and the value of the air and shipping services which use the air and waterways of the Arab world are fairly well understood. Since the War, too, United States strategic interest in the area has become equally urgent. For, concurrently with the development of the great oil fields in the Arabian Peninsula, there has been a decline in the strength and influence of Britain, forcing the United States to assume the defense responsibilities for this classic target of Russian aspirations. It is not surprising, therefore, that the United States should take an active interest in the Anglo-Egyptian Suez Canal controversy, in French policies and actions in North Africa, in the so-called Middle East Command and its various substitutes, and in the Arab-Israeli struggle. In the absence of an independent American policy, these interests have led the United States to align itself with Britain and France, against whom the Arabs are continuing their struggle for independence. At the same time, the influence of the local American scene on American foreign policy has hoodwinked American policy-makers into espousing the cause of Israel, and has so far thwarted all efforts to disengage American Arab policy from that of Israel. Until the United States acquires a policy of her own for the Arab world, it must continue to be considered an obstacle to Arab aims and aspirations.

The "cold war" has also highlighted Russia's role in the affairs of the Arab world. In spite of the fact that the Russian Revolution of 1917 has brought to an end direct Russian dealings with the area, Russia remains a current factor in all Arab policies and actions. Russia, it will be remembered, was a party to the Sykes-Picot Agreement. Czarist Russia's ambitions in the area have never been renounced by its Soviet heirs. Soviet Russia, too, has been one of the original supporters of the Partition of Palestine and a steady source of arms for Israel. It thrives on disruption and chaos, and aspires to supplant the West throughout the area.

VIII. Religious Minorities

IN THE ARAB world are many religious minorities, the most important of which are the Christians—including their divers sects Eastern and Western—the Jews, the Sabians, and several sects which have branched off from Islam itself, such as the Druze, the Nusayris, and the Alawites. There are also national minorities such as the Kurds, the Turks, the Berbers, the Negroes, and the Circassians. Furthermore there are other groups which are at once religious and national, such as the Yazidis, the Assyrians, and the Armenians in the east, and the French, Italians, and Spaniards in the west. Nevertheless, the problem of minorities, whether religious or national, does not appear uniformly in manner, extent, or gravity in all Arab countries. Some Arab countries, such as Saudi Arabia and the Arab countries of the Persian Gulf where the bulk of the population is Arab and Moslem, hardly know what the problem of minorities is. Others, such as Lebanon, Iraq, Algeria, and Morocco, face the problem with all its concrete implications and consequences.

The appearance of these religious and national minorities in the Arab world was natural. For the Arab East has been the cradle of all revealed religions, and in its different countries these religions have split into sects. The Arab East was also a highway over which from time immemorial different peoples crossed as merchants and as conquerors, and a refuge to which others fled for security and protection. When in the seventh century the Arabs emerged from their Peninsula as conquerors, preaching a new faith, many non-Arabs flocked to Islam, gradually through intermarriage became intermixed with the conquerors, and eventually became Arabized. The Arabs, however, did not force their religion upon the peoples of the conquered territories. For the most part those who embraced the new religion did so freely. Some accepted Islam from conviction, while others did so for convenience, hoping to reap the earthly benefits accruing to its adherents or to enjoy the advantages and privileges it bestowed upon its followers. But there remained within the new Moslem world many who held fast to their faith and preserved their national identity and their own language. By and large, it is these peoples who constitute today the religious and national minorities in the Arab world. Others settled in the region, either as conquerors or as refugees, long after the Moslem conquests of the seventh century, and even in modern times. Still others branched off from Islam itself and sought refuge for themselves and for their schismatic beliefs from the persecution of the Sunnite majority in the fastnesses of the area, particularly the mountainous regions of the Lebanon and Syria.

Throughout the Moslem period, these religious and national minorities were able, on the whole, to preserve their own identities and to pursue their religious practices freely. Tribal spirit and local pride enhanced their loyalty to their faith, particularly since these religious beliefs were the symbol of their unity and the outward expression of that provincialism which they jealously treasured and were ever ready to defend.

The primary concern of the various Moslem states was, generally, to defend their territories from outside attacks, maintain internal public security, and collect the taxes. Otherwise, those minorities were left free to earn their living, transact their business, and manage their national and religious affairs. Each religious sect had its own hierarchy, which ruled its religious affairs and regulated its family life and relations. Furthermore, these minorities, and particularly those who lived in remote and isolated places, were better able to preserve their local autonomy and to retain their particular languages, religions, and rites because poor means of communication and difficulties of movement from one place to another usually confined the authority of the central government to accessible population centers. For this reason the central government depended on feudal lords and religious heads to extend its control over remote regions. Likewise, it often exploited sectarian divisions to reinforce its power, setting one faction against another and using the one to subdue the other.

Not all of these minorities were able to remain completely isolated and to preserve their racial, religious, and linguistic identities. Those living in the midst of Moslem Arab majorities became, in time, Arabic-speaking and, under the influence of Arab culture, became to a large extent Arabized. Even their ethics, mores, and moral values became, in spite of the religious difference, almost indistinguishable from those of their Moslem neighbors. This is evident among most of the Christian communities in the Arab world—the Copts of Egypt, the Maronites of the Lebanon, and the other Christian sects in Palestine, Syria, and Iraq.

Nor did the Ottomans attempt to bring into being a unified and homogeneous state. Rather they left religious and national differences as they were. This seeming tolerance or policy of laissez faire toward the various religious and national groups within the empire stemmed initially from the Moslem tradition of noncompulsion and from Ottoman unconcern so long as these minorities paid their taxes, observed the law, and abstained from disturbing public order and security. But in time this tolerant attitude towards religious and racial differences became one of the underlying principles of Ottoman policy of "divide and rule," and the instrument with which the Sultans were able to keep their hold upon their far-flung empire. To that end they aroused Moslem against Christian, Sunnite against Shiite, Kurd against Armenian, Eastern Orthodox against Latin, etc. Withal, the Ottomans maintained the Moslem practice towards non-Moslem subjects *(rayahs)* of granting them the right of governing their own religious and personal affairs. These rights of the various religious groups were legally defined and regulated through the *millah* system. The legal status of each *millah* (religious group, sect, nationality), and its rights and duties were spelled out through various edicts promulgated during the nineteenth century under the influence of the "European Concert." The most important of these edicts were the *Hatti-Sherif of Gulhane* (1839), the *Hatti-Humayun* (1856), and the Ottoman Constitution of 1876.

These regulations, which were formulated for the purpose of defining the status of each *millah,* fortified the autonomy of each, strengthened the bonds among its individual members, accentuated the spirit of separatism among them, and increased the power of their hierarchies, feudal lords, and influential men.

When the foreign powers began to encroach upon the sovereignty of the Ottoman empire, particularly since the beginning of the eighteenth century, and to extend their influence over its internal life, they found in these minority groups extremely convenient instruments. Each foreign power, therefore, adopted a *millah,* proclaimed itself a protector of its interests and a defender of its rights, and proceeded, under the guise of this protection, to intervene in the internal affairs of the empire. As a result, the Ottoman empire itself began to grant these groups special privileges, often under duress. France adopted the Maronites and the Latins, Russia the Eastern Orthodox. Since the close of the nineteenth century, Austria and Italy had embraced the Greek Catholics and the other Christian groups acknowledging the supremacy of Rome. Britain displayed special interest in the Druze in particular, and in the Moslems in general, whenever the Moslems were in need of the support of a foreign power.

The means by which the foreign powers extended their influence over religious minority groups included schools and institutions wherein the language and the culture of the particular power were imparted, and at times religious missions which preached the love of their sponsors along with the love of Christ. Intervention on behalf of these groups in the internal affairs of the empire usually took place through diplomatic channels, open and secret, and at times, through direct military and political action, as in the case of the Lebanon in 1840 and 1860.

107

Foreign intervention on behalf of these religious groups accomplished an improvement in their status, strengthened their position in the empire, and increased the measure of their autonomy. Nevertheless, it aroused against them the ire of the Ottomans and the resentment of the Moslem majority. Moslems looked upon these minorities with suspicion, and considered them a disturbing factor in the community and a tool in the hands of foreign politicians, constituting a grave danger to the state in particular and to Islam and Moslems in general. What made matters worse and increased popular rancor were these minorities' fancy for European culture, their preference for European mores, the collaboration of some of them with foreign powers, and the use made of the talents of some of their members by the foreign powers in their consular services and their religious, educational, and commercial institutions. It should also be pointed out that the employment by members of these minority groups of Western methods and techniques in commerce and industry has naturally enabled them to surpass their Moslem neighbors in business success, and has therefore increased Moslem resentment and intensified the feeling among Moslems that these minorities are competing with them and crowding them out in their own countries.

The special status which these religious minorities enjoyed for centuries made of them isolated social groups leading a semi-independent life within the borders of the various Arab countries, self-contained and hypersensitive, inordinately jealous for their own interests, suspicious of the surrounding Moslem majority, and constantly feeling that their life in these countries and among these people bordered on a sojourn in an alien land. The fact that the Moslem majority, from the earliest days of the Islamic state, has been accustomed to look at non-Moslem groups with suspicion, condescension, and studied indifference, mixed in most cases with contempt and in some cases with violent molestation, accentuated their isolationist tendencies, their self-containment, and their apprehensions. When in recent times, the national and liberation movement got under way, it was inevitable that it should suffer, among the factors of confusion, backwardness, and discord, this profound cleavage between the Moslem majority and the minority groups, dividing the latter's loyalty between the particular sect to which each minority belonged and the country wherein it lived. This problem was rendered more acute and complicated by the Mandate powers during the period of their mandate over most of the Arab countries.

When Iraq, Palestine, and Transjordan fell under the British mandate and Syria and Lebanon under the French, both Britain and France proceeded to strengthen the spirit of sectarianism, to accentuate religious dissensions, and to give sectarianism the added impetus of vested interests. Backed by the League of Nations, which was proclaiming the safeguard of minority rights and the preservation of their autonomous existence, these religious minorities, in Iraq, came to enjoy individual representation in parliament, and the Iraqi government gave official recognition to their hierarchies, ecclesiastical councils, and laws regarding personal status.[1] In Syria, France consolidated the foundations of sectarianism by dividing the country into four petty states along sectarian lines. In Lebanon the whole fabric of representative government, parliamentary and municipal, had sectarian bases, as did the distribution of governmental positions. France justified its action on the grounds of equity among all sects, the safeguard of their rights, and the preservation of their historical autonomies. Consequently, sectarianism in Lebanon has become one of its most complicated problems and the basic cause of most of its crises and instability.

There is no doubt that the problem of sectarianism in Lebanon is old, antedating the French mandate. Each one of its sects has lived for a very long period in isolation, self-contained, clinging to its own traditions, suspicious and apprehensive of the other sects. The feudal system which prevailed in the Lebanon, the inordinate influence and power wielded by its religious leaders over all aspects of its social, economic, and political life, and the general ignorance of the majority of its people constantly sharpened sectarian cleavages and added to the heritage of ill will among the members of the various sects. In 1860 the enmity produced by all these factors culminated in the bloody massacres of Christians by the Druze and the Moslems in Dayr al-Qamar, Beirut, Hasbayya, Zahlah, and Damascus. These massacres left deep scars on the minds of the Christians—painful and frighful memories which the years have not yet been able to erase. Religious sects have long lived in the Lebanon, hostile one to another and fearful one of the other. Each looked for a foreign power to defend and support it. The role played by the French mandate was to emphasize these dissensions and to fan their flames. Consequently all governmental rules, regulations, laws, and institutions stressed and buttressed sectarian cleavages. Parochial schools, whether native or foreign, have also nourished the spirit of sectarianism, while feudal lords, opportunistic newspapermen, and merchants of politics have tried to defend it on the basis of logic, justice, and national interest; and religious leaders have not ceased giving it their blessing and continued support. Besides other social, political, and economic factors, this spirit of sectarianism and the deep-rooted (and not always unjustifiable) fear on the part of minority groups of the Moslem majority are the main incentives which drive some influential Lebanese to cling fast to Lebanese independence from other Arab countries, strengthen the separatist spirit, and lure them to attempt the transformation of Lebanon into a national home for the Christians of the Arab East.[2]

While discussing religious minorities and the spirit of sectarianism, mention should be made of the divisive feelings existing between the two great Moslem sects: the Shiites and the Sunnites, particularly in Iraq. They made their appearance long ago when revolutionary Shiism struck out against established Sunnite rule. The traditional rivalry between the Ottoman and the Persian empires, which were fighting, among other things, for hegemony over Iraq, complicated the situation still further. When finally the Ottomans prevailed and extended their rule over Iraq, they favored the Sunnites and

110

depended upon them for the consolidation of Ottoman rule; at the same time they persecuted the Shiites, neglected the education of their children, did nothing to improve their social and economic status, and refrained from employing their talents in the administration of the country. The spirit of sectarianism resulting from these factors and from a general ignorance of the spirit of Islam in particular should have gradually disappeared with the advent of national government in Iraq, mainly by doing away with its political, social, and psychological bases by re-educating the people and directing them towards a common loyalty based upon equality of all citizens, by inculcating the spirit of good citizenship among them, and by guiding them out of their narrow sectarian isolation to the common bond of nationalism. The Mandate power, however, feared a unified Iraq, and therefore followed a policy designed to perpetuate these differences and to invigorate the spirit of sectarianism. Support was given to feudal lords, religious leaders, and opportunistic educated men, all of whom saw in the preservation of the status quo the best safeguard for their threatened influence. Sectarianism became a vested interest. It still remains an obstacle thwarting almost every effort to improve the economic and social conditions of the country, and a bone of contention diverting the attention of the populace from basic problems to a constant jockeying for influence and position by the two conflicting sects.

It was reasonable to expect that recent developments in the Arab world, including the modern means of communication which have firmly linked its various parts, the rise of modern governments, and the spread of education, would lead to the weakening of the spirit of sectarianism, if not to its eradication. But other factors, old and new, real and artificial, were at work entrenching and strengthening it. The most important of these were the policies and actions of the foreign powers, the work of the missionary and parochial schools, and the activities of some secular and religious leaders who were interested in the continuation of sectarianism for the preservation of their position, influence, and privilege. Consequently, sectarianism, while not existing legally in most of the Arab countries, has become concretely established in the life of the people, among both the Moslem majority and the various religious minority groups. It exists in spite of official denials by rulers, political leaders, and religious heads, and in spite of repeated protestations by them concerning the unity of the nation, the singleness of its purpose, and the oneness of its goal. Rather these denials of sectarianism are an evidence of its existence and perhaps a sign of its gravity.

The problem of religious minorities and its sectarian corollary were briefly traced in their historical context merely to determine the factors which have given rise to them. In the past, when the state was theocratic, based on religion, and when the loyalty of the individual was first and foremost to the particular denomination to which he belonged, sectarianism was a natural thing. Today, however, it has become unnatural, contrary to the evolutionary law, opposed to the torrent of nationalism which engulfs the Arab world, incompatible with the spirit of liberation, independence, and progress. Sectarianism dissipates national effort, drains its vitality, and diverts its attention from fundamental issues. It cuts up every Arab society into fragmentary social islands, self-contained, hating one another and hostile one to another. It creates among the individuals of these fragmentary social islands a narrow spirit completely inimical to patriotism. For the person whose thinking is incapable of transcending the horizon of his own sect cannot develop any feeling for the welfare of the country in general. He does not feel that strong bond which should hold all the individual members of the country and impel them to work for the good of the nation as a whole. Furthermore, sectarianism sacrifices the rights of the majority of the members of the group for the benefit of a few feudal lords, politicians, religious leaders, and opportunists in general. It throws away the rights of segments of society and retards their progress. Confessional sectarianism, like tribal fanaticism, is an anachronistic vestige of the past, which negates nationalism and its prerequisite of undivided loyalty to the fatherland.

The main problems of the Arab world today are liberation from foreign domination and matching other countries in economic, social, and cultural progress. Neither is attainable unless the Arabs first unite, and then co-ordinate their national aims and policies. For this reason sectarianism constitutes one of the major obstacles in the path of unity, and in turn in the path of liberation and progress. When it is also remembered that among the most important impediments to Arab co-operation and unity is the absence of any conscious national feeling among the Arab masses which would induce Arab governments to strive for Arab unity, the danger of sectarianism and its influence in weakening national consciousness and obstructing its growth become evident. Sectarianism is, therefore, one of the major divisive factors among the Arabs today, to say nothing of the blatant attempts of some of its advocates to separate and isolate their countries from other Arab countries in order to preserve their sectarian entities and personal interests. Amidst the hubbub of sectarianism, its cunning maneuvers, and smouldering hates the voice of Arab nationalism is lost, the battle cry for Arab liberation is drowned, and the general welfare of the Arab fatherland is submerged.

IX. National Minorities

THERE ARE MANY non-Arab racial elements in the Arab world. Some of them, such as the Kurds and the Berbers, were there long before the Arabs themselves. They continue to live in clustered groups, and hold fast to their own traditions and languages. Of late, the educated among them have begun to develop strong national consciousness, and to strive to secure for their people rights equal to those of the Arab majority. It is those segments of the population which shall be discussed under the heading of national minorities.

Until the end of the nineteenth century the Arab world had no such thing as a national minority problem. People knew nothing of the meaning of nationalism, and had no clear national consciousness. To the average individual, the *millah* was at once the religious group to which he belonged and the national home wherein he lived. On the other hand, Islam, as a universal religion, made no distinction between one people and another, and entertained no preference for one color over another. Nationalism in its Western connotation first reached the Arab world towards the end of the nineteenth century, and did not take form until the period preceding the First World War, when Ottoman hostility to national and religious minorities was intensified. With the rise of the Society of Unity and Progress, the idea took a more definite form, and reached its full development after the influence of the foreign powers had penetrated the Ottoman empire, and more particularly after these foreign powers had seized, after the First World War, the Arab countries formerly under Ottoman rule.

The Arab world continues to face these national minority problems. The situation is further complicated by the failure of the Arab governments and the Arab national movements themselves to gain a correct understanding of the problem, their refusal to recognize that any national minority is entitled to any rights, and the exploitation of the legitimate demands of those minorities by their own leaders and by unscrupulous opportunists among them, who would sacrifice those demands for their own personal influence and benefit. Racial fanaticism, therefore, has become, like sectarian fanaticism, an instrument to dissipate the vitality of the people, exploit popular issues, and help individuals to reach governmental high office. The foreign powers used racialism as they used sectarianism—to divide the population in order to consolidate power and control over the country. In Iraq, Britain used the Kurdish, Yazidis, and Assyrian problems to push the country into constant strife and bloody feuds which cost the government and the people, including the minorities themselves, thousands of lives and enormous effort. Until 1953, Britain used the problems of the African tribes in the Sudan to sever the southern part from the northern, to obstruct the independence movement, and to forestall any possible unity with Egypt.

114

In North Africa, the French are using the Berbers to destroy the unity of the people in their struggle against French colonialism. The case-histories of two minorities, the Kurds and the Berbers, provide examples.

THE KURDS IN IRAQ

In general, the Kurds inhabit the mountainous region extending along the Iranian-Turkish-Iraqi border, to the southwest of the Caspian Sea. The Kurds of Iraq inhabit the northeastern provinces between the eastern borders of Iraq and a line extending through the mountainous region from Zakh east of Erbil to Kirkuk. Although scholars have not determined their origin with certainty, the Kurds are generally thought to be an Aryan people. Some scholars, however, assign to them a Turanian origin, asserting that they are descended from the Turanian tribes mentioned in the Assyrian records under the name of Gurdu or Kurdu, and inhabiting the mountain ranges in the north of Assyria. With the destruction of Nineveh and the disappearance of the Assyrian power, these tribes supposedly became intermixed with the Medes and became Aryanized. Their language, which resembles Persian, is considered an offshoot of the Aryan.

The Kurds form the largest national minority in Iraq, and number about 800,000.[1] They are divided into many tribes, some of which are still nomadic, while the majority live in villages where they pursue farming and cattle raising. A few live in cities as artisans, others are employed in government offices or serve in the Iraqi armed forces. They are represented in almost all Iraqi cities.

Until recently, the tribal feeling among the Kurds was much stronger than the nationalist. Even today the nationalist spirit in those country regions removed from the centers of political activity is still weak. New factors, however, have arisen which have unified Kurdish feeling and brought about a strong national consciousness among them. Among these factors is the movement of many Kurds to cities, where they have formed a new bourgeois class engaged in industry and

115

trade-pursuits which they consistently shunned in the past. Another factor is the increase in the number of educated Kurds. During the Ottoman period, their education was for the most part Turkish, and since the advent of the Arab rule it has become either Arab or Western. A few of the educated Kurds have allowed themselves to be assimilated into these two cultures—the Turkish and the Arabic—but the majority have remained loyal to their national culture and tradition, and have striven to develop and promote it anew. They have been instrumental in reviving Kurdish literature and have carried out an intensive literary activity among the Kurds of al-Sulaymaniyyah and Bagdad, at the same time keeping in touch with other Kurdish centers in Turkey and Syria. At present they are endeavoring to revive Kurdish national consciousness and promote the idea of Kurdish unity and independence,[2] particularly by pointing out to their fellow Kurds the administrative ills and social injustices they are suffering under foreign domination. Kurdish public opinion and national consciousness have been further strengthened, especially since the end of the Second World War, by the political events which took place in the Kurdish region in Iran, where the Kurds were able to disengage themselves from Iranian domination and constitute a Kurdish republic in Mahabad, not far from the Iraqi borders, although that republic was short-lived.[3]

At the end of the First World War, the Kurds launched their demands for the establishment of a Kurdish state in the Kurdish regions formerly under Ottoman rule. Kurdish societies which were organized in Cairo and Constantinople established contact with the Supreme Allied Council in Paris and succeeded in persuading it to acknowledge the right of the Kurds to form an independent state. The Treaty of Sèvres, which Ottoman Turkey signed on August 10, 1920, stressed this right and recognized in Article 64 the rights of the Kurds who inhabited "that part of Kurdistan which has hitherto been included in the Mosul vilayet" to form an independent state if a majority of the population desired independence.[4]

Neither the Allies nor the Kemalist Turks, however, abided by this principle, and the Treaty of Lausanne made no mention of Kurdish independence. The new Turkish government, having disposed of its internal problems and strengthened its position by its victory over the Greeks, retained its control over the Kurds within its domains and stood firm against the establishment of an independent Kurdish state which might become a danger threatening its back door. Consequently the Kurdish problem in Iraq developed into an internal problem with which Iraq alone was concerned. Furthermore, although the Treaty of Sèvres was never implemented, it left a deep impression on the minds of the Iraqi Kurds who aspired to independence, and strengthened their faith in the justice of their cause. As a result, the Kurdish problem played an important role in the life of Iraq, and has occupied the government and the people from the day the national government was established until the present time. The Kurds have not ceased to demand internal reform, autonomy, and even complete independence. They have staged several revolutions, the most important of which were the successive uprisings of Sheikh Mahmud in the Sulaymaniyyah province, the insurrections of Sheikh Ahmad al-Barazani during the period of the mandate, and the revolutions of Sheikh Mustafa al-Barazani after the Second World War. The British authorities in Iraq often incited the Kurds against the Iraqi administration, particularly whenever Britain wished to secure Iraqi agreement on some political move and whenever it desired to intimidate the nationalists. The successive Kurdish insurrections, in which the lives of thousands on both the government and the rebel sides were lost, retarded the peaceful development of the Kurds in Iraq. The constant protests and demands for independence and equality with which the Kurds showered the Iraqi government, as well as the British Residence in Bagdad and the League of Nations at Geneva, secured at least some of the Kurdish national aspirations. The Iraqi government gave the Kurds schools where the language of instruction was Kurdish and courts where cases were presented and tried in Kurdish,

117

threw the civil service open to Kurdish officials, facilitated for Kurdish youth entry to all government schools and colleges in Bagdad, and pushed through economic, social, and administrative reforms in the Kurdish regions almost exceeding those carried out in the Arab regions, although in both the Arab and the Kurdish regions those reforms fall short of the needs of the population and the requirements of modern times.

The situation in Iraqi Kurdistan is at present quiet, at least on the surface. The early revolutionaries occupy high positions in the government—as cabinet members, deputies, senators, and senior officials in governmental bureaus. Most of them have settled down in Bagdad, where they have become accustomed to luxurious urban life. They have allied themselves with the government: many of them now prefer to be ministers, deputies, and senior officials in a large state, the capital of which is Bagdad, to being leaders of a small state of limited area, old and dilapidated towns, and meager bounties. Nevertheless some of them still exploit the Kurdish problem, every now and then protesting Kurdish grievances in order to bolster their influence among the Kurdish masses and to frighten the central government into granting what they desire. On the other hand, the government has been successful in winning over to its side a large number of feudal lords, aghas, and influential chieftains. It has strengthened their positions, fortified their power, and increased their wealth, thereby alienating the common people and intensifying their discontent. Consequently, divers political movements with different aims and methods have cropped up, particularly among the educated Kurds. Although these movements are for the most part secret and usually operate underground, their influence is spreading among the Kurds. Perhaps the most notable among them are the Communists, who have gained in influence and number since the Second World War. The Communist line reiterates that the principal cause for the deplorable conditions of the Kurds in Iraq and for their desperately depressed standard of living and bad administration is to be found in British influence and its tools and allies, the

118

local reactionaries. The Communist agitators further state that Kurdish aspiration will not be attained until all popular forces, Kurd and Arab alike, unite to destroy their common ills: backwardness, poverty, and oppression. After Iraq is finally freed of all foreign influence and local reactionary control, the Kurds will then decide whether they want independence or autonomy within the state of Iraq, or continue to remain, as they are at present, citizens of Iraq. On the other hand, the strong Kurdish nationalists, known in Iraq as the separatists, call for complete independence and demand the immediate introduction of democratic institutions and of far-reaching social and economic reforms.

The Berbers of North Africa

The Berbers are the original inhabitants of North Africa, and have lived there since the earliest times. Anthropologists are not agreed on the race from which they were descended, and linguistic scholars are not unanimous on the origin of their language. Some anthropologists hold that they were descended from two peoples of dark complexion, one from the non-Negroid peoples of the African Desert and the other from southern Europe. To these two was added a small white element from northern Europe. As for their language, some scholars maintain that it is akin to the Hamitic Kushite, which has close relations with the Semitic family of languages.

For long centuries the Berbers have lived along the stretch which extends from Tripolitania to the Atlantic and from the Mediterranean to the borders of the Great African Desert. They have constantly resisted the inroads of foreign influences brought by successive waves of conquests. Even the most important of these conquests, the Phoenician, Greek, Vandal, and Roman, failed to leave a noticeable influence upon the indigenous inhabitants. Divided into numerous tribes, to which they were fanatically loyal, they were unable to unite into a single nation except for short periods before the Arab conquest.

With the Arab conquest many of the Berbers embraced Islam and took part in completing the conquest of North

119

Africa and then Spain. They supplied the new empire with some brilliant generals, of whom the most important was Tariq ibn-Ziyad, the conqueror of Spain. The Arabs, however, were unable to leave any marked and basic influence upon the Berbers either racially or linguistically throughout the first three centuries following the conquest, primarily because the invaders were comparatively few in number and because they settled in the main cities and in military garrisons while the Berbers remained removed from the invaders and inhabited in general the mountainous and desert regions and the countryside. But the immigration of the banu-Hilal around the middle of the eleventh Christian century to North Africa brought about a basic and a profound change in the national substructure of the Berbers. The banu-Hilal spread throughout the area and intermixed freely with the native population. Gradually the Berbers inhabiting the cities, the plains, and the hills were Arabized, discarding their customs, forgetting their language, and adopting Arabic as their vernacular. In time they became for all practical purposes Arabs. The only segments of the Berber population who held fast to their national characteristics and continued to speak the native language were the inhabitants of the remote fastnesses of the mountains and the desert, and those from the plains and the hills who chose to join them. These Berbers were later able to establish strong dynasties which succeeded in subjugating a large portion of North Africa and Moslem Spain for a fairly long period of time. Among those were the Almoravids, the Almohades, and the Marinids. After the downfall of the various Islamic states and the decay of Arab civilization in the West, the Berber tribes broke up and were scattered. Likewise they forgot a great deal of Islam and its teachings. The majority of the Berbers retained only the rudiments of the faith. But a few pious men of Almoravids endeavored during the fifteenth and the sixteenth centuries to revive Islam and restore its doctrines and practices among the tribes.

At present, the majority of the Berbers are in Morocco, where they inhabit the Atlas Mountains, and in particular the

Riff, where they constitute 60 per cent of the population. A large portion inhabits the Algerian mountains and hills. The most important are the Kabyles hills, and to their southeast the Aures. In these areas the Berbers constitute 29 per cent of the population. A small number live in Tunisia and in Mount Nafusa in Tripolitania, while a few are scattered around the oasis of Siwa in the Libyan desert. In other words, the Berber concentration increases in intensity as one moves from Tunisia westward to Morocco and from the Mediterranean southward to the Great African Desert.

The Berbers in these areas have preserved their racial characteristics and their language. The language itself is more or less primitive, and is divided into many distinct dialects, in which the influence of Arabic is noticeable, both in vocabulary and in structure. The literature is for the most part primitive, drawn from the literatures of other peoples, and is unwritten but transmitted orally from generation to generation. The Berbers also preserve many of the ancient customs and traditions, some of which may be traced back to pagan times. Many of the practices concerned with daily transactions and personal status do not conform to Islamic doctrine and usage.

In consolidating their colonial rule over North Africa, the French made great use of the Berber situation, and created from it a major problem which they added to the many obstacles they had already raised in the path of the Arab liberation movement. They have methodically followed a policy of "divide and rule" among the two peoples, the Arabs and the Berbers, particularly by encouraging Christian missionary activity among the Berbers in the hope of weaning them away from the Arab Moslems. They have also stressed among the Berbers the fact that they were a separate people, totally distinct from the Arab invader. They have likewise made use of the theories which hold that the Berbers were of European descent, in order to impress upon them that they were really Europeans, and that their spiritual contacts and relations should, therefore, be with the Europeans. They have urged the Berbers to turn their eyes toward Europe, the cradle of their ancestors, and more particularly toward France, and to sever whatever relations they may have had with the East, especially with the Arabs. The French have also striven to revive Berber customs, traditions, and usage, and have drawn upon them as a source for civil legislation in order to strengthen the separatist trend among the Berbers, weaken the hold of Islam upon them, and thereby widen the cleavage between them and the Moslem Arabs. Mention has already been made of the so-called al-Zahir al-Barbari,[5] perhaps the most flagrant of those divisive measures. Tribal organizations were likewise strengthened and tribal chiefs supported and cajoled, thereby making them natural allies of French colonialism and a ready instrument to thwart every national or liberation movement.[6]

The cleavage between Arab and Berber in North Africa, strengthened by the French in every manner possible, diverts the vitality and effort of the people to undesired channels, weakens the liberation movement, and forces it to emphasize the religious appeal. This religious appeal, which has become the last remaining bond between Arab and Berber, has rendered the national movement in North Africa different from the other and purer nationalist movements in the Arab world.

Side by side with this problem is that of the foreign *colons,* of whom there are in North Africa about two million—French, Spanish, and Italians. They control the political and economic life of the area and direct its educational and cultural development. The presence of these *colons,* who are not at all likely to be assimilated into the majority and become Arabized, complicates the liberation movement in North Africa still further. To safeguard their vested interests they are most anxious to perpetuate and to invigorate French and Spanish power and influence. They see in the independence of the area a weakening of their position, a limitation of their privileges, and a threat to their very existence. Consequently, they employ the power they possess over the administration and the control they have over the economic life of the area to accelerate the processes of assimilation into French and Spanish life, and to

122

isolate the area as much as possible from any contact with the rest of the Arab world. It is these *colons* who generally dictate French North African policy.

The Arabs' first and foremost problem is to liberate their fatherland from foreign domination of whatever form and to rid themselves of all social and economic institutions which have stood in the path of their progress and reduced them to the status of backward and disunited peoples. Neither liberation nor progress is, however, possible without the concerted will of the people, Arab and non-Arab, Moslem and non-Moslem, to liberty and progress. Above all, no individual is likely to give his loyalty to any country and to co-operate with his fellow citizens unless he feels that, within that country, he has the same rights and the same duties as any other citizen, irrespective of race, color, or creed.

The situation, therefore, would require that the Arabs, now striving for the liberation and progress of their fatherland, should neither discriminate against nor persecute the national minorities which have been living in their midst from earliest times. The situation would also require that if the various national movements at work in the Arab world truly desire to solve the complicated problems of their fatherland, and enlist the co-operation of all its citizens, and to allay the fears of the minorities which dread the possibility of being engulfed and swallowed up by the Arab majority, these national movements should then make a special effort to understand the aspirations of the minorities, recognize their legitimate and natural rights, and accord their members absolute equality with other citizens.

X. Diversity of Political Aims

THE ARAB WORLD today is a world of confusion, divided as it is into areas in which local conditions vary widely; and wrenched by the conflicting interests of feudal families, ambitious political men, different social classes, foreign powers who seek their own aims, and arbitrary local governments. Above all, the concept of nationalism is still new and not fully developed or crystallized among many of those engaged in the national movement. Differences in their regional, religious, and social backgrounds lead inevitably to differences in their understanding of Arab national aims, and in turn to a difference in the methods they employ for the achievement of those aims. In view of all these considerations, the diversity of Arab political aims and methods would seem indeed natural. The diversity has more than one important aspect: provincialism and the anti-nationalism of the Neo-Shu'ubiyyah movement and of certain Islamic tendencies. These will be discussed at length below.

1. PROVINCIALISM

Arab provincialism may be described as the feeling among the inhabitants of one Arab country that it is their only homeland, that they should be proud of it and promote its independence, and that the inhabitants of other Arab countries, though Arabs like them, are so remote that there is no need to become united with them. It is even more accurate to state that the idea of union does not enter their thinking.

The Arab world is divided into a number of provincial divisions, or regions, or countries, or states. Although they share the general Arab character, these provincial divisions differ one from the other. The difference is slight in adjacent countries and extensive in the distant ones. The distinctive features of the different areas are neither superficial nor accidental.

In the first place, geography, already discussed in the second chapter, has divided the Arab world into regions separated by extensive deserts or high and inaccessible mountains, such as the Syrian desert which separates Syria from Iraq, the desert which separates the eastern coastlands of the Peninsula from the western, and the Lebanon and Anti-Lebanon ranges which separate the Syrian littoral from the interior. In the past, this geographic factor was reinforced by primitive means of communication. Consequently every provincial division was exposed to particular conditions, fell under particular influences, and gradually acquired particular characteristics. What was true of the larger provincial divisions was also true of the smaller divisions. Each small region within a country acquired distinctive characteristics. These, however, are now fast disappearing because of improved communications and because of the rise of modern central governments, the development of economic life, and the spread of modern and unified systems of education. The speed with which the differences within an individual country are disappearing, however, exceeds the speed with which the differences between the different Arab countries are disappearing.

Besides geography, another factor has left its divisive mark on the Arab world. For these various provincial divisions were inhabited, before the Arab conquest, by various peoples, each having its own language or dialect, its own literary heritage, its own religion, superstitions, and folklore, its own social customs and traditions, and its own ethnic make-up. When these peoples became intermixed with the Arab conquerors and were eventually Arabized, they did not lose all their ethnic characteristics or all their psychological and social make-up. In fact, the Arabs gave to every people with whom they became intermixed their general characteristics and received from every one some elements of its own, vaguely discernible at times, and at times clear. This is evident in the different facial features seen among the Arabs, the different manner of speech, the various vernacular dialects, the distinctive social customs, and the accumulated intellectual sediments. The vernacular dialects of the Arabs differ from one country to another because of many influences, not least important of which is the fact that the peoples who inhabited these parts did not speak a common language or dialect. Spoken Arabic was, therefore, influenced by the dialects of the pre-Arab inhabitants. The Syrian dialect, for example, has been influenced by the Aramaic and its various dialects which were spoken in Syria before the Arab conquest, in word-formation, derivation, conjugation, pronunciation, sentence construction, and particularly vocabulary. Similarly, the North African Arabic dialect has been influenced by the Berber dialects spoken in the area. Furthermore, the Arabs did not settle in equal numbers in every provincial division and region. Wherever they settled in considerable numbers, the Arab characteristics are more numerous and clearer. Again, every Arab country is influenced by adjacent countries and by the states which governed it after the fall of the Arab administrations. Iraq, for example, was more influenced by the Turks and the Persians than by any other nation because of its close proximity to both, and because both, particularly the Turks, governed it for a long period of time after the fall of the Mongols. The Arabs of North Africa, on the other hand, were not influenced by the Turks to any perceptible degree but were directly influenced by the Spaniards and the Portuguese, who governed parts of North Africa during different periods subsequent to the Arab evacuation of the Iberian Peninsula, and who had extensive commercial contacts with North Africa. In addition Arab refugees brought along with them Spanish and Portuguese influences. The Arabs of North Africa were influenced by the French, Spaniards, and Italians who have swarmed into the area as immigrants, merchants, and conquerors, since the latter part of the eighteenth century.

Religion, too, with its rituals and traditions, has left a deep mark on some provincial divisions of the Arab world and has given each of them distinctive characteristics. A Christian, born, say, at Kasirwan in the Lebanon, would surely feel lost if he were moved to the austere desert simplicity and Moslem sternness of Mecca or al-Najaf—he would have absorbed all the influences of the Maronite Christian atmosphere—with churches and shrines, icons and statues of Christ, the Virgin, and the saints, priests and monks to direct his steps and ages-old Maronite practices to prescribe his manner of living. In his home place church bells peal out their chimes at the early hours of the dew-soaked morn to awaken the villages from their slumber at hilltops and along mountain slopes, and the dusk creeps somberly through the yawning valleys to envelop the mountains with its dark mantle and draw the faithful into

126

tender reveries which conjure up in their souls ecstasies of bliss and tranquil hope. Such are the contrasts of the Arab world.

Differences of custom, and of mode and standard of living, have given each Arab country its own provincial character, and have made the inhabitants of each feel that they are a distinct unit, closely bound together but not closely linked to the inhabitants of the other Arab countries. Furthermore, these social and geographic factors have been strengthened by several political influences which continue to emphasize the provincial outlook. During the Omayyad and early Abbasid periods, the Arab world was divided into administrative provinces almost identical with the present divisions. When, almost a century after its rise, the Abbasid state began to show signs of weakness, petty states arose in most of the Arab countries, bound to the central government by nothing beyond the nominal recognition of the Caliph. In some cases even the nominal recognition of the Caliph was brusquely thrown overboard. Indeed, the Arab world never knew what complete unity was, except during short periods prior to the end of the second Moslem century. Even then the empire was decentralized and not strong in political unity. Each one of the petty states left its particular stamp upon the region it occupied, and bequeathed to it its architectural monuments and cultural remains and the memories of its military exploits and disasters. All these have left prominent marks on the history of each provincial division.

The divisions which befell the Arab world after the collapse of the Abbasid Caliphate, and more particularly, after the Ottoman occupation, were more important and their influence on the spirit of provincialism more far-reaching than any previous divisions. Iraq and Syria fell under Ottoman control towards the middle of the sixteenth century, and remained subject to the Turks until the end of the First World War. Only the Lebanon enjoyed a certain measure of autonomy and local administration, particularly after the middle of the nineteenth century. Before that time it had been governed by princes nominally subject to the Sublime Porte but in practice independent. The most important of these dynasties were the Ma'nids and the Shihabids. At the same time (1516), Egypt fell, nominally, under the domination of the Ottomans, but continued to be governed, in actual practice, by the various Mameluke dynasties. It disengaged itself still further from Ottoman control and became practically independent of the Caliphate during the early years of the nineteenth century, when Mohammed 'Ali established himself as master of its destiny. In the Peninsula, Ottoman control remained nominal and confined to particular regions, namely those adjacent to Iraq and Syria. Otherwise, the Peninsula maintained its practical independence, owing allegiance to numerous petty dynasties of sheikhs, emirs, and imams. Morocco remained under the rule of the Alawite dynasty from the beginning of the tenth century until the French and Spanish occupations during the early years of the twentieth. In fact the Alawites are still the nominal rulers of Morocco legally, although they have lost all the prerogatives of government under the protectorate. Algeria, Tunisia, and what is now Libya were nominally subject to the Ottomans, but in actual practice independent, ruled by various petty dynasts: deys in Algeria, beys in Tunisia, and the Karamanlids in the Libyan littoral.

When Western colonization came, it confirmed these divisions, froze the status quo, and actually increased the divisions of the Arab world by creating political units which had never existed before. France and Spain first, and then Italy, proceeded to consolidate their rule over North Africa and to isolate it as completely as possible from the eastern parts of the Arab world. The area, which at least officially formed a unit under the Ottomans, was dismembered into kingdoms, emirates, and mandates, each a political entity with artificial boundaries, and a ruling dynasty. These divisions, which were conjured into being during the nineteenth century, were perhaps the most serious elements in consolidating provincialism and invigorating its spirit. Each Arab country became politically distinct and separate from the others, while economic and

128

cultural life in each assumed a different orientation. In every one of these newly constituted countries there grew up a ruling class concerned with preserving provincialism, maintaining the independence of its country from the other Arab countries, guarding its interests, and perpetuating its power and control over the area. Consciously and unconsciously, it strove to create and to strengthen the spirit of provincialism among the people. This trend is further abetted by those elements whose interests lie in keeping the Arab world divided and by those who sincerely see in the existing provincial divisions historic foundations and authority, affirmed and vindicated by the special features and characteristics of the provincial division and its people and by the actual present.

It might be pointed out that the political divisions which came into being during the nineteenth century have been stressed and given more importance in the development of the provincial spirit than those which appeared in the Arab world after the end of the second Moslem century. The reason for this emphasis becomes apparent when it is recalled that the concept of the modern state did not reach the Arab world until the nineteenth century. Previous to that time, the prevailing concept was the religious; and Islam, nationality, and patriotism were indistinguishable. The religious bond was at the same time the national bond and the patriotic bond. As far as the individual was concerned, his "national" or "patriotic" feeling did not go beyond his village, town, or tribe. The idea of the nation, national consciousness, and citizenship, or the feeling of the individual that he was an individual member of a large fatherland, did not enter into the consciousness of the Arab. Nor did he feel much different when one Moslem state displaced another in the region where he lived or when the boundaries of his particular country were extended or diminished. Now, however, the modern Arab states, through the new administrative systems and regulations they have introduced and the improvements they have brought in communications and in the economic and educational life of their respective countries, have created in every single country, besides political unity, what amounts almost to economic and cultural unity. The individual is now brought up with the feeling that the country in which he lives is his own homeland, the state is his state, and the nation is his nation. Everything around him conspires to augment this feeling: his government, the boundaries of his country from which he cannot make an exit without a passport, the school where he receives his education, and the newspaper which he reads. Consequently, to think of the Arab movement as a whole, or Arab unity, and of the Arabs as one nation which could or should be a single state or at least a federation of united states has become something requiring special training and a specific national education. Had Transjordan, for example, not been carved out of Syria and constituted by the British a separate emirate, the present inhabitants of the region east of the Jordan would not have become accustomed to deem themselves Jordanians but would have developed the feeling that they were Syrians.

In this manner provincialism became an actual reality, clear and alive in the consciousness of the individual Arab, or at least in the consciousness of the professional politician. This provincial consciousness is further strengthened by various movements rising in almost every single Arab country and demanding that provincial status quos be recognized and preserved. Some are clearly opposed to the Arab movement and champion provincialism, attempting to consolidate it on historic grounds other than Arab and resorting in consequence to the history of those peoples who inhabited the area before the Arab conquest. The most important of these anti-Arab movements will be discussed later. In the meantime mention should be made here of the rise of widespread movements, alternating between vigor and weakness, which call for the literary use of the provincial colloquial tongue and the discarding of the classical Arabic, on the ground that the colloquial language is closer to the native tendencies of the people and more indicative of its spirit and national outlook. This language is furthermore supposed to be a more resilient instrument of expression, conveying ideas to the reader in a natural, simple, warm, and direct manner, just as they were conceived in the mind of their author, without being dulled and delayed by the classical style, which requires thought and deliberation on the part of its user. These movements are not infrequently met in Egypt, Lebanon, and Algeria, for example, but they are limited in scope and are weak, if not actually on their way out. Although they have stirred up in the past, and more particularly during the fourth decade of the twentieth century, a war of words between their proponents and those of the classical, and have revived provincial shibboleths and local fanaticisms, they have found little favor among the larger public and have been unable to withstand the classical current. It is noteworthy that the proponents of the colloquial languages themselves employed the classical in their campaign.

What attitude have the national and patriotic movements taken toward provincialism? Arab patriotic movements in general and nationalist movements in particular are of very recent beginnings. They did not appear until after contacts between the Arab East and the conquering West were established. When these movements gained consciousness, they found provincialism an actuality. Necessarily, the national movements assumed the form of the provincial. Furthermore, the national movements had to face the various problems of local provincialism: struggle against foreign occupations, resistance to existing governments, demands for constitutional, social, and economic reforms, etc. Because of these factors, and because of the absence of direct contact between the various Arab countries as a result of colonial domination and existing local governments, the majority of these national movements have been diverted from the major Arab cause to lesser local causes. To wrest the independence of their particular country from the foreigner, guard its boundaries and its security, and reform its conditions became the chief concern of political movements in every Arab country. Their most effective weapon was to instill a local national consciousness in the minds of the people, remind them of their past and present accomplishments, and arouse their patriotic sentiment in every possible

131

way. The people were quicker to respond to immediate and urgent problems than to far-off aspirations removed from their understanding and remote in fulfilment.

The national movement appeared in Egypt before it appeared in the other Arab countries. From the days of Mohammed 'Ali, when Egypt acquired a definite political status, the movement followed a line of development independent of the other Arab countries. Egypt was preoccupied with its own internal affairs, and, since 1882, with the problem of British occupation and with its relation to the Sudan. These two problems absorbed all the attention and efforts of Egypt and gave it little opportunity to concern itself with the fortunes and misfortunes of the other Arab countries. Actually, the national movement in Egypt has always followed an orientation largely Egyptian and Islamic rather than Arab. It did not emerge from its isolationism and embrace the Arab cause in a clear and effective manner until the fourth decade of this century. Nevertheless, the Islamic and Egyptian character of the movement still prevails. The same is true of the national movements in North Africa, whose distinguishing features continue to be their struggle against colonialism, their Islamic character, and their clearly provincial nature.

Indeed, the Arab national movement did not assume a general Arab character except in certain parts of the Arab world and only during a specific period of time. These parts were limited to Iraq and Syria, while the period was confined to the early years of the twentieth century when the area was under the Ottomans and was engaged in a struggle against it. At that time the individual in these countries was better known as an Arab than as an Iraqi or a Syrian or a Palestinian. More accurately, he was known as a Bagdadid, a Mosulid, a Beirutid, a Jerusalemite, or an Allepoite. When the Arab world was divided into several countries after the First World War, the struggle against foreign occupation preoccupied the national leaders, and perforce the major Arab movement received only a fragment of their attention. In spite of that, Arab feeling in Iraq and Syria remained strong, and the idea of Arab unity and Arab co-operation is stronger there than in the other Arab countries.

For a period of time, the national movement, which has started in a strong manner in the Arab world, was overtaken by weakness, only to become invigorated again since the Second World War. It was destined, however, to collide with the spirit of provincialism, which had already become crystallized and more deeply entrenched in popular consciousness, and, in some regions, had been transformed into narrow provincial chauvinism.

This section has been devoted to the forces which make for provincialism. In previous chapters the factors which prepare Arabs to transcend the provincial feeling and to embrace the idea of the larger Arab fatherland have been discussed. All these factors, whether those which help to broaden the national horizons of the individual Arab or those which narrow them to the limits of the smaller country wherein he lives, are at work simultaneously, competing for his loyalty. Nevertheless, no matter how strong the factors of provincialism may be, the factors of unity among the Arabs are as strong if not stronger. No matter how deep the provincial character may be, the general Arab character is deeper. In fact the forces working for unity have left their clear impressions upon the various national movements, and have begun to orient those movements more and more towards the general Arab point of view. Foremost among these factors of unity are the increased inter-Arab cultural, economic, and national contacts, the growth of Arab national consciousness, the surge of liberation movements, and the compact of the colonial powers against the Arab world. These factors prompt the Arabs to a feeling of common fate, and force them to co-operation and unity for self-defense and -preservation. The League of Arab States has failed to solve many of the Arab problems. Its weakness and ineffectiveness in the face of danger has become apparent. But in spite of all that, it has served the Arab idea by placing it before the Arabs in a practical way. It has introduced into the consciousness of the Arabs the fact that the problems of the Arab world are interdependent, and that they cannot be solved except as a whole, through concerted action, complete co-operation, and unity.

2. The Neo-Shu-ʿubiyyah

Besides the provincialism we have seen, a further force against Arab unity is the countertendency to Islamic resurgence called the Neo-Shuʿubiyyah.

During the early Abbasid period, frustrated Persians launched the so-called Shuʿubiyyah movement in order to thwart their Arab rulers. A literary campaign to vilify the Arabs, disparage their history, belittle their intellectual heritage, and deny their role in the creation of Islamic civilization was carried out by the proponents of the movement. Their basic aim was to weaken Islam, which has destroyed the Persian empire and humiliated Persian national pride, by weakening the Arabs, the mainstay and standard-bearers of Islam in those days. The new movements to be discussed in this section have been collectively termed Neo-Shuʿubiyyah, because they are in essence a reaction, conscious or unconscious, against the Islamic awakening and possible Islamic resurgence, and against those national movements which the advocates of the Neo-Shuʿubiyyah deem either synonymous with Islam or a disguise under which it masquerades.

The Islamic awakening did not come about spontaneously, nor was it without far-reaching results which have left a deep impression upon the thinking of educated Arabs in general—Moslems and non-Moslems alike. It came about as a response to the challenge of Western powers to the Moslem Arabs: the invasion of their lands by Western colonialism politically, economically, and culturally.

Reaction to this Islamic awakening and to the factors which brought it about assumed divers forms. Modern educated Arabs, many of whom were Christians, particularly of the Lebanon, pursued an Arab nationalist direction. They endeavored to restore the Arab intellectual heritage, to revive Arabic and its literature, and they called upon their fellow

Arabs to awake and regain their former glory, and to guard it against the ruling Turks on the one hand and against the colonial inroads of the West on the other. At times, these thinking Arabs followed clearly secular lines, while at other times their endeavors were unable to do so. It is nevertheless a fact that many of the standard-bearers of Arab nationalism and the revivers of the ancient Arab heritage during the latter part of the nineteenth and the early part of the twentieth centuries were Christians from the Lebanon and Syria, who saw in nationalism a possible instrument not only for breaking away from Ottoman domination, but also for breaking through the constraining shell of Islam into a larger and more spacious milieu wherein both Moslem and non-Moslem could lose themselves in one all-inclusive loyalty.

Several educated Arab groups, particularly Christian ones, however, could not lend themselves to this Arab nationalist trend, primarily because they were not and could not be sure that Arab nationalism would pursue a clearly secular direction. In fact they doubted the ability of Arab nationalism ever to be independent of religion. They viewed it as a thin veil for Islam, the resurgence of which they dreaded either because of fanaticism or because of time-honored and historic fears, sometimes genuine and often artificial and imagined, or because of a sincere belief that religion has become obsolete and could no longer serve as a basis for a firm and progressive national structure in these modern times. The movements of these educated groups assumed divers forms—ideological and political—of which the most important were Pharaonism in Egypt, Phoenicianism, the Culture of the Mediterranean Basin, and the Syrian National Socialism in Lebanon. Directly and indirectly Western colonialism invigorated these movements through its many schools in the Arab world, particularly in Lebanon, and through its press and some of its Western writers and orientalists.

a. PHARAONISM

At the time the Islamic awakening was unfolding with vigor in Egypt, the idea of Arab nationalism was being spread

135

and promoted in Egypt by Syrian and Lebanese journalists and thinkers who found refuge there from the Hamidian terror. Also the British were beginning the consolidation of their occupation. Simultaneously, archaeologists were entering upon the golden age of Egyptology, uncovering the buried treasures of the land, and publishing the results of their learned labors, which depicted the ancient glories of Egyptian culture and civilization. Egyptian civilization was described in superlative language, not befitting staid scholars, as the earliest of all civilizations and the fountainhead of all subsequent accomplishments. It was both inevitable and natural that these momentous discoveries should leave a deep impression upon the minds of educated Egyptian youth, stir their patriotic feelings, and arouse their national pride. Popular admiration of Pharaonic civilization expressed itself in many ways ranging from unbridled delusions of grandeur to sober and well-reasoned appreciation.

Admiration of Pharaonic culture and civilization, which was to develop later into the Pharaonic movement (initially a sort of phil-Pharaonic trend), assumed a vigorous character among modern educated Egyptians, particularly the Copts, among whom the movement gained momentum after the assassination of Butrus Ghali Pasha,[1] on February 20, 1910, at the hands of an irresponsible fanatic who could not tolerate the idea of a Christian in the post of the prime minister. The spread of the Pharaonic idea was further promoted by the fact that the majority of the modern educated Egyptian Moslems were then offspring of Turkish families which had settled in Egypt and become Egyptians only in name. These Egyptians of Turkish descent despised the Arabs and disliked the budding Arab movement because of its potential threat to Turkish hegemony. At the same time the phil-Pharaonics were preaching that Egypt was essentially Pharaonic and that the Egyptians still retained the heritage of their Pharaonic forebears in bodily structure, facial form, as well as psychological makeup, emotional predilections, and social customs. When compared with the Pharaonic, the Arab influence

136

among the Egyptians was, according to those phil-Pharaonics, superficial. They, therefore, stressed the need for the restoration of the Pharaonic tradition, the revival of ancient Egyptian literature, and the development of modern Egyptian literature in accordance with the ideas and models of the ancient. They called for the glorification of Pharaonic Egypt, its great Pharaohs, and its immortal deities, and for breaking away from the Arabs and their civilization. They insisted that Egypt has its own particular humanistic, cultural, and educational entity, and that it was not linked to the other Arab countries except through weak and tenuous bonds, the most important of which was religion. Religion was, however, in the process of receding from social life in these modern times, and language alone would not make those who speak it a nation.

The movement stirred up a great hubbub and a vociferous ideological war which did not subside, in spite of the paucity of the number of "combatants," until the forties of the twentieth century, primarily because of the influence of those combatants in Egyptian literary and intellectual circles and because of the violent reaction it caused in Islamic and Arab society within Egypt and without. For some time, therefore, nationalist Arabs and those involved in Arab problems in general looked upon Egypt with grave suspicion and mistrust in all matters pertaining to Arab nationalism.

British colonialism fed and encouraged this movement, both morally and otherwise, in order to weaken and splinter nationalist forces and divert their efforts away from the Moslem and Arab worlds. Nevertheless this Pharaonic movement seems to have spent itself and died since the beginning of the fourth decade of the century. Several reasons contributed to its decay. Foremost among these was the weakness of its historical and ideological foundations. Also instrumental were the vigor of the nationalist movement, the growth of national consciousness, and the vitality of the Islamic awakening which, in the mind of the majority of the Egyptian public, cannot be separated from the Arab. There was finally the change in

137

Egyptian policy which brought Egypt closer to the other Arab countries, especially during and after the Second World War. All these factors have restrained the excesses of many of the advocates of phil-Pharaonism and led them into other directions, either Arab or Islamic or moderately Egyptian. Others too became preoccupied with current political movements and modern economic and social problems.

Sober and well-reasoned appreciation of Pharaonic Egypt, however, found a firm place in Egyptian intellectual life and became part of the contemporary Egyptian scene. The glories of ancient Egypt were exploited by political leaders, writers, and poets to bestir the Egyptian masses who have been bowed down by long centuries of deprivation, ignorance, poverty, and oppression, and to restore their self-confidence and national dignity. Ancient Egyptian civilization has been cited to refute British insinuations that the present-day Egyptians are backward and incapable of progress. Interest of Egyptians in their ancient history could also be discerned in the numerous literary and scholarly works which treat of the cultural accomplishments of the ancient Egyptians and which are offered as part of the required curriculum in Egyptian schools and as reading material for the educated; in the museums which the governments maintain especially for ancient remains; in the facilities offered for visiting the ancient monuments wherever they may be; in the artistic trends through which young Egyptian artists are trying to imitate and to revive the methods and norms of Pharaonic art; and in the preference which the wealthy show, in decorating and furnishing their sumptuous homes, for artistic objects, motifs, and paintings depicting the life of ancient Egyptian society.

Side by side with the clear and strong Islamic orientation and the growing nationalist Arab trend, there is in Egypt today a strong bent towards taking pride in the Pharaonic heritage and considering it one of the living factors which have fashioned the Egyptian people and molded their mentality. This bent, which is being inculcated in the minds of the modern Egyptians with a considerable degree of insistence and continuity, is among the factors which give Egypt, besides its general Arab character, a distinct character of its own, and strengthens the trend towards a pure Egyptian nationalism which acknowledges its link with the Arabs, and glories in Arabism, but considers itself above all a separate and an independent entity. For a symbol of its modern awakening, Egypt has adopted the picture of an Egyptian peasant woman shaking the Sphinx out of its dreaming slumber. The Sphinx represents ancient Egypt and typifies its deep and mysterious spirit. The junta government which took over the affairs of Egypt after the coup d'etat of July, 1952, has recently issued new paper currency bearing on the obverse the likeness of one of the great Pharaohs and on the reverse the picture of a mosque surrounded by the lotus plant, the sacred floral emblem of ancient Egypt. It also issued a new set of postal stamps, one bearing the likeness of the Sphinx, a second bearing that of Nefertiti, and a third that of Tutankhamen. Even 'Ali Mahir,[2] President of the Arab Federation in Egypt, in an address analyzing the principle underlying the coup d'etat of July 23-26, 1952, was not immune to the Pharaonic influence and inspiration. In an apologia, delivered on November 14 of the same year, he said, ". . . Divers aims have prompted those successive awakenings . . . but in their totality, they were resounding cries in the face of despotism and tyranny of whatever source or origin, and indelible proofs that the heritage of the time-honored cultures and great civilizations still flows in our lifeblood, and that the millions of Egyptians are heirs of that glory which rises firmly on the banks of the Nile, the handiwork of the mighty Pharaohs and the glorious Arabs."[3] Similarly, Taha Husayn, in an article inspired by the same coup d'etat and entitled "An Awakening," states, ". . . We were wont to exert our utmost and expend the limit of effort to make the Egyptians feel that their fatherland never tolerated oppression, never cringed before disaster, and never submitted to aggression. We were wont to repeat these things to the Egyptians to restore to them self-confidence, and to the foreigners to regain their confidence in Egypt and compel them to respect it again. We were wont to pursue Egyptian history to ancient times only to discover that Egypt had revolted against the Persians, giving them no rest and itself not resting until it was rid of them. Likewise it revolted against the Macedonians, giving them no rest and itself not resting until it Egyptianized them. Henceforth, it proceeded to Egyptianize every foreign invader until each became an Egyptian, and then forge out of its naturalized children instruments for the attainment of its independence. This Egypt has done throughout its different ages. Consequently it preserved its identity, and never dissolved into a small nation or an imperious enemy, but rather dissolved into itself every invader and everyone which attempted to exploit or colonize it."[4]

b. PHOENICIANISM AND THE CULTURE OF THE MEDITERRANEAN BASIN

A second strain in the Neo-Shu'ubiyyah is Phoenicianism. The proponents of Phoenicianism and the Culture of the Mediterranean Basin assert that the Lebanese are not racially Arabs but Phoenicians, and that their culture is that of the Mediterranean Basin. They regard the Lebanese as not related to the Arabs or linked to them except through language. The idea did not appear publicly until after the Syrian Revolt (1925-1927), when it began to spread in some circles. It remained for several years a subject for parlor discussions and table talk. Its inception, however, dates from the beginning of the French mandate over Lebanon. For no sooner had France been granted the mandate over Syria and Lebanon than it proceeded to pursue a different policy with each. Its Syrian policy aimed at weakening what it considered the stronghold of resistance, while its Lebanese policy aimed at strengthening what it considered the citadel of co-operation. Thereupon Le Grand Liban came into being, and, overnight, four independent Senjaks emerged within Syria. Notwithstanding this policy of dismemberment, the fear that the area might unite prompted the government under the mandate to seek a firmer foundation for its presence. The phil-Pharaonic idea had already appeared in Egypt a little earlier. And it was from Egypt that the French received the inspiration to contrive a parallel separatist movement which would draw upon the ancient historical lore of their favored Lebanon. A few years later Mussolini raised the cry of *"mare nostrum,"* claiming that the Mediterranean was first and foremost an Italian sea. To further his idea in the early thirties of the century, he founded a society for the promotion of its culture, the Mediterranean Culture. The proponents of Phoenicianism seized upon the idea in order to buttress the weak foundations of their own ideological edifice. At the instigation of the mandate government, its intellectual janissaries proceeded to develop the idea as a basis for severing Lebanon from the Arab family. Around the middle of the thirties, the idea, fully developed and adorned with all the paraphernalia of scholarship, was presented in book form.[5] Its advocates endeavored to show that Lebanon possessed its own distinctive character, and they began to call for its complete separation from the rest of the Arab world. They sang in classical Arabic verse and prose of the greatness of the Phoenicians and of their glorious accomplishments, in works such as Sa'id 'Aql's *Qadmus* ("Cadmus"), and tried to promote the use of the local Lebanese colloquial as the sole literary language. The movement met with some limited success among particular groups, the majority of whom were educated Christians who had received their training at Jesuit schools. The chief basis for its success was the mistaken idea that the Arabs today have two opposite orientations: the Desert and the East on the one hand and the Mediterranean and the West on the other. The separatist groups feared that the Arabs would choose the Desert-East orientation. Having failed to draw the majority to their movement, the separatists resumed their efforts with added vigor by indirect and oblique methods. They asserted that the Arab world was being torn between two ideologies: democracy in Lebanon and theocracy in the other Arab countries. Lebanon, they further stated, has always had its peculiar and distinctive

141

characters—a part of the West in the East. They then turned to the development of their separatist ideas through a series of public lectures designed to strengthen the trend which *Ta'rikh Lubnan al-Mujaz* had tried to set. The fact is, however, that the Arabs have never set their eyes towards the Desert-East at all, and that all indications are that they would never turn eastward either in the near or remote future. Since they emerged from the Desert thirteen centuries ago, the Arabs have set their faces towards the West, not the East. In fact the Desert has had no palpable influence upon their culture, civilization, or political and social trends since the fourth Moslem Caliph 'Ali moved his capital from Medina to al-Kufah in southern Iraq. When they overran the Fertile Crescent and Egypt and inherited their cultures, they entered universal history. They also entered the Mediterranean Basin, and its culture became their culture.

The historical basis of Phoenicianism merits little attention. In spite of their penetration to some of the interior centers of commerce, the Phoenicians had settled the coastland, not the mountains, which were then covered with thick forests and formed a shelter for wild beasts and a hiding place for brigands. Furthermore, every attempt to build nationalism on the basis of race is doomed to failure, since racial purity is nonexistent, even among the primitive tribes of central Africa. It is therefore ridiculous to assert its existence in a place which has been a melting pot for races, wherein the blood of the Arab conquerors had been intermingled with that of the indigenous population, and where, besides their blood, those Arabs gave the conquered people their language, culture, literature, and social institutions.

The Culture of the Mediterranean Basin is sometimes instanced to support reasons for isolating one Arab country from another. But is there really a culture which is Arab, another which is Islamic, still another which is European, and so on? There are in the world today three main and living cultures or civilizations: the Chinese, the Indic, and a third to which the rest of the civilized world belongs.[6] This third civilization is a mixture of different elements which have been intermingled over and over again. In the mixture of these elements lies the secret of its strength and vigor. Of these elements some are Egyptian, some are Sumerian, and others are Babylonian, or Greek, or Roman, or Arab. It would therefore be incorrect to designate the civilization by the name of any of the component elements, and it would be impossible to call it pagan, or Jewish, or Christian, or Islamic. While every one of these designations would bring out one of its many attributes, none is sufficient or comprehensive enough to describe it in its entirety. The most suitable name for that civilization would seem to be that of the Mediterranean Basin, not so much because the Mediterranean Basin was its birthplace as because it was the place where its different elements became intermixed, and where the civilization itself developed and reached its maturity. The Mediterranean Basin, too, possesses a geographic, commercial, social, and cultural unity. Its culture is a blend of three component parts: Greek thought, Roman law, and Semitic religion. Each one of these is, in turn, composed of diverse elements, to the development of which different peoples contributed.

In the seventh century, the Arabs made their entry upon the stage of universal history by the destruction of the Sassanian empire and the near destruction of the Byzantine, from which they wrested its richest provinces. Subsequently, they contested the hold of Constantinople and Rome over the navigation and commerce of the Mediterranean Sea, and succeeded in gaining control over it. In so doing, the Arabs, contrary to Pirenne's view,[7] did not destroy the economic and cultural unity of the Mediterranean world but strengthened it, and the Mediterranean became and remained from the eighth to the eleventh century an Arab sea. During that period they spread throughout its Basin what they had inherited from the Byzantines and the Egyptians and what they received from the Jews, Christians, and pagans of Harran. In other words, the Arabs became the standard-bearers of the Culture of the Mediterranean Basin, enriched it by their own contributions, and car-

143

ried it to the different parts of their far-flung empire, from Spain in the West to the confines of China in the East, and from the Caspian Sea in the North to the sources of the Nile in the South. The Arabs seized control over the navigation of the Mediterranean and made it an Arab sea, but they were vanquished by its culture. They readily and enthusiastically entered into its service and raised for it beacons of light in Bagdad, Damascus, Cairo, Tunis; in the principal cities of Spain, in Toledo, Cordova, and Seville; and in southern Italy and Sicily. These became centers for the dissemination of its material and nonmaterial elements. The role which the Arabs thus played was the same role as that played by those who had preceded them in the Mediterranean Basin. In fact the Arabs did not enter universal history until they had left the Desert and come into the Mediterranean Basin and adopted its culture and civilization. The logic of the facts, therefore, dictates that the Arabs be recognized as an integral part of the Culture of the Mediterranean Basin and a very important factor in its development and preservation. The Culture of the Mediterranean Basin offers no grounds for the separation of the Arabs from other Western peoples in culture and civilization. Nor does it offer any grounds for separating one Arab country from another in that respect.[8]

c. The National Socialist Movement
(The National Syrian Party)

The National Socialist Movement, which will be treated briefly, is the most vigorous movement opposed to Arab nationalism. It is also the clearest in its aims and the strongest in its organization. While the movements just discussed represent ideological programs the activities of which are confined to the field of thought, and which employ the written and the spoken word for gaining popular support, the National Socialist Movement has combined thought and organized political action in its operations. The founder of the movement was Anton Sa'adah, who brought his program into being when he organized the National Syrian Party in Lebanon during the early thirties of the twentieth century.

Basically, this movement does not differ from the other nationalist movements which appeared both in Europe and the East. Like them it emphasizes the verity of the nation; its unity, which is the result of a long history; its interest, which is above all other interests; and its single society, which is united in interest, goal, and feeling. It therefore rejects, at least theoretically, all divisive sectarian cleavages and all narrow provincial divisions. It does not recognize class and other concepts common among bourgeois national movements. The new element in the movement is its assertion of the existence of a particular Syrian nationalism independent of the Arab. In fact this is the central doctrine of the movement and the axis around which it revolves. Several French writers, particularly the famous Jesuit Orientalist, Father Henri Lammens, in his book *Syria* expounded and promoted the idea some years before Sa'adah.

According to Sa'adah, the Syrians form a distinct nation. The Syrian movement exists by itself, completely independent of any other movement. The Syrian nation rests on the unity of the Syrian people, and emanates from a long national existence going as far back as prehistory. The Syrian fatherland is the natural habitat in which the Syrian nation developed. Its geographic boundaries, which distinguish it from other fatherlands, extend from the Taurus Mountains in the northwest to the Bakhtiyari Mountains in the northeast, the Suez Canal and the Red Sea (including the Sinaitic Peninsula and the Gulf of Akaba) in the south, the Syrian Sea (including Cyprus in the west, and the Arabian Desert and the Persian Gulf in the east. Sa'adah referred to it in a general term: "the Fertile Crescent and its star, Cyprus."[9]

Sa'adah bases his movement on the premise that the Syrians constitute one complete nation, unrelated to the Arab nation except by tenuous bonds, the most important one of which is language. He also holds that what is referred to as the Arab nation is in reality nonexistent. There are, however, divers

145

peoples who speak Arabic, but who are socially, economically, and intellectually different. The Syrian nation has come into being within the full light of history, and has preserved its independent personality and identity in spite of numerous conquests. The Arab conquest left hardly any influence upon it. On the contrary, it was Syria which has left its influence upon the conquering Arabs, impressed upon them its particular character, and melted them in the crucible of its entity. He further maintains that the Arabs are a race distinct from the Syrians and inferior to them in vitality and culture. When the Arabs entered Syria they did not bring with them Arab civilization; on the contrary the Arab civilization was merely a fusion of Syrian and other civilizations. "The Yarmuk[10] was the door through which the Arabs entered Syria, but never a door for Arab civilization. The civilization of those peoples who entered the Mohammedan pale of Islam, sometimes designated on the basis of language as 'the Arab civilization,' was in reality the civilization of the Syrians, Persians, and Greeks in the Arabic language."[11] It was Sa'adah's practice often to indulge in the praise of the past of those peoples who had settled Syria, like the Phoenicians and the Aramaeans, and to laud their advanced culture, initiative, and enterprise. At the same time he was always fond of attacking the idea of Arabism, Arab nationalism, and the Arabs in general. In this connection, Sati' al-Husari states, "I have come to know that the primary motive (for those attacks) was Sa'adah's misunderstanding of the real meaning of the terms 'Arabism' and 'Arab nationalism.' I have clearly noticed that the idea of Arabism was constantly confused in the mind of Anton Sa'adah with desert nomadism on the one hand and with Mohammedan fanaticism on the other. The man had imagined that the idea of Arab unity was nothing but a veil behind which the partisans of Islamic sectarianism hid. Consequently he attacked this sectarianism, as he was wont to attack all sectarianisms in general. This was the 'leaven of error' which permeated the mind of Sa'adah with its ferment, and corrupted his scientific, social, and political thinking."[12]

146

According to Sa'adah, the cause of the Syrian nation should become independent of that of the Arab nation, since the latter will inevitably be lost, and it has caused the Syrian nation a great injury by retarding its development and robbing it of many of its characteristic elements and much of its vitality. Furthermore, this unfortunate link has cost the Syrians part of the Syrian fatherland. On this point he says, "I had no doubt at all that Arabism—the Arabism of 'the Arab father-land,' which extends like a long tape, irregular and meander-ing, around the coastlands of West Asia and North Africa; and the Arabism of 'the Arab nation,' which is found among different and divided racial groups, conflicting environments, and dissimilar mentalities; and the Arabism of 'Arab society,' which lacks all the characteristics of a true, living, and active society and all the factors of a united social order; and the Arabism of the forty or fifty million Arabs—is a lost cause in Syria. It dissipates every effort on the part of the Syrian nation to preserve its entity, safeguard its fatherland, and realize its aspirations to life. I have come to the conclusion, after a thorough study of the mentality of that Arabism in Syria— the mentality of Arab nationalism—that it was a psychological disease which has distorted and disfigured the Syrian mind, perception, and logic."[13] Nevertheless, Sa'adah was unable to deny altogether the bonds which exist among the Arab countries, or to ignore the benefits which they might reap from co-operation. He, therefore, has advocated inter-Arab co-operation, though only after Syria had raised itself to a position of leadership in the co-operative front. That front, however, would not be formed of peoples belonging to one nation, but of peoples of similar interests. "The existing order in the Arab world is one of nations and societies the co-operation of which is easy. It is, therefore, feasible to form of them a co-operative front. That order, however, is not one of a single nation or a single society. Syria must first raise itself in order to be able to concern itself with the affairs of the Arab world and in order to be an active force in the forma-tion of the Arab front."[14]

It is not the purpose of this study to refute the arguments upon which the National Socialist Movement has been built, but rather to indicate the extent of its influence in increasing dissension among the Arab countries and in hampering the development of the idea of co-operation among them, particularly in Lebanon, where National Socialism met with considerable success. Part of this success was the result of the strong personality of its leader and the almost religious faith his followers had in him. More important, however, were the deep-rooted enmity toward Arabism and Islam among many Lebanese, and the spade-work which Phoenicianism and the idea of the Culture of the Mediterranean Basin had done in preparing the minds of a considerable number of Lebanese for the acceptance of National Socialism. Furthermore, a portion of Lebanese youth, dissatisfied with destructive sectarianism and narrow provincialism, and at the same time rankling with resentment against Arabism and Islam—or fearful of them—found comfort in the movement and saw in it a political ideology which might fulfill their aspirations. National Socialism, side by side with Phoenicianism and narrow provincialism, which dominate the minds of few Lebanese—like the Phalanges (al-Kata'ib), who believe in a particular Lebanese nationalism and a Lebanese independence that should be guarded against any form of Arab co-operation or unity—played a very important role in alienating people from the idea of Arab nationalism and co-operation, and in preoccupying them with issues which have no bases in history, and are removed from the true actualities of Arab life: the struggle for liberation from foreign colonialism and local tyranny, and for the improvement of Arab life economically, socially, and culturally.

In Syria, to which the public party activity was transferred after the execution of Sa'adah (July 9, 1949), the success of the movement was meager. Nothing is more indicative of this than the fact that the National Socialists in Syria embraced the coup d'etat of December 19, 1949,* and supported it, consider-

---

* That of Adib al-Shishakli.

148

ing it a part of their movement. Initially, the authors of the coup d'etat seemed to favor the movement and did actually make use of some of its membership. Before long, however, they declared their loyalty to Arabism and their belief in Arab nationalism and Arab unity, and consequently founded The Arab Liberation Party (Hizb al-Tahrir al-'Arabi). Whether or not they were sincere in their protestation of loyalty to the Arab cause is not important. What is important and noteworthy is that they were prompted to found the party because the general Syrian public is devoutly Moslem and fanatically Arab, steadfast in its loyalty to its Arab heritage, and keenly conscious of the bonds of brotherhood which link it to fellow Arabs in all Arab countries.

In Iraq, "the Eastern wing of Syria" according to the National Socialists, the movement met with nothing but the ridicule of the few who got to know its underlying principles. For the Iraqi is capable of understanding that he is an Iraqi, because he lives in Iraq; that he is an Arab, because he belongs to the Arab nation and partakes of its common culture and heritage. But he cannot in any way understand that he is a Syrian or a Syriac simply because a group of individuals want him to be so.

These movements which are opposed to the Arabs and to Arab nationalism have contributed to the creation of a political babel in Syria and Lebanon, have sown the seeds of dissension among Arab youth, and have caused the dissipation of much energy in resisting their inroads, refuting their arguments, and deflecting their attacks. These efforts could have been better spent in the struggle against colonialism and in combatting the forces of backwardness and disintegration in the Arab world. On the other hand, these movements have rendered a great service to the cause of Arab nationalism. They have stirred Arab nationalists from their apathy, warned them of the necessity for clarifying their aims and unifying their forces, and have impressed upon them the importance of coordinated and positive action among the rank and file of the Arab public.

3. ARABISM AND ISLAMISM

Arab national movements and Islamic movements agree on many points and disagree on others. They meet on some of the immediate and long-range aims and part company on some. This agreement between national and Islamic movements stems from the nature of Islam itself and from the nature of Arab nationalism. For with the advent of the Prophet Mohammed and his Islamic mission the Arabs entered upon the stage of universal history, acquired historical importance as a nation, and participated actively and in a worth-while manner in enriching the cultural heritage of mankind. If the Moslems regard Mohammed as the greatest and the last of all prophets, the Arabs regard him as their national hero and the greatest man ever to appear among them. If the Moslems hold the Koran sacred because it is the revealed word of God, the Arabs consider it the ideal in Arabic literary achievement, the norm which writers should approximate, and the faithful guardian which preserved their language pure and saved it from melting away into the various provincial colloquial languages, in spite of the collapse of Arab hegemony and the rise of foreign domination. If the Moslems glory in Islamic civilization, the Arabs are equally proud of it, because it was, for the most part, the result of Arab genius acting through the medium of the Arabic language. If the Moslems honor the memory of their illustrious caliphs and distinguished men, the Arabs honor them too because they were Arabs. Furthermore, since Arabic is the language of Islam and the Koran, Moslem regard for it has extended to everything Arab and to every individual Arab, Moslem or non-Moslem, who has rendered a service to Arabic, enriched it with his intellectual contribution, and helped promote Arab culture. As a matter of fact, the Moslem Arabs addressed themselves to the study of pre-Islamic poetry, collecting it into anthologies, writing commentaries in explanation of it, and setting it up as a model for emulation in form and content, even when the authors were unbelieving pagans—whose religious beliefs Islam was determined to eradicate. The Christian faith of al-Akhtal did

150

not worry them when they admired his poetry. Nor did they take any notice of the religious faith of Hunayn ibn-Ishaq (a Nestorian), Thabit ibn-Qurrah (a pagan star-worshipper), and Musa ibn-Maymun (Maimonides, a Jewish rabbi), when they read and studied these scholars' writings and their translations from Greek. On the contrary, they have accorded them the honor they deserved as leaders in the Arab intellectual heritage. From the beginning, Islamism and Arabism have been organically intertwined in such a way as to make it almost impossible to separate the one from the other. It is impossible to separate 'Omar, genius of Arab politics and administration, from 'Omar the Moslem caliph and generalissimo of the Moslem conquests, or 'Ali, the paragon of Arabic eloquence, from 'Ali, the Moslem martyr.

In more recent history, too, Islamism and Arabism have been organically intertwined to such an extent that it is almost impossible to separate the one from the other in the mind of the Moslem Arab public. The modern Arab awakening has been a part of the general Moslem awakening in the nineteenth century. Husayn ibn-'Ali, the national Arab hero of modern times, the leader of the Great Arab Revolt against the Turks, and the prime mover for the establishment of a unified Arab state, was, as a Moslem figure, the Custodian of the Two Harams, the Sharif of Mecca, and the descendant of the Prophet, declared by some the Caliph over all Moslems.

Nevertheless there is a basic difference between the modern Islamic movements and the Arab national movements. The national movements, in general, rest on the premise that the Arabs are one nation, distinguished from others by peculiar characteristics. They advocate Arab unity, and desire to erect their state upon modern and secular foundations, independent of religion. They also advocate the employment of all that is useful in modern civilization—its science, methods, means of production, and economic and social systems. These movements glorify the illustrious Moslem Arabs who were instrumental in producing the ancient Moslem Arab heritage because that heritage is Arab, and because those who produced it were for the most part Arabs.

Throughout this investigation, mention has been made of the Arab national *movements* rather than the Arab national *movement*. This is because, in reality, there has not existed in the Arab world any single national movement with a single program and a single aim. On the contrary, there are several national movements which agree on some points and disagree on others. Some still betray a strong Islamic character. Others are more truly nationalist, but advocate that same simple and vague Arab nationalism which was advocated by Arab youth prior to the First World War—namely, that which limited its program to the independence and unification of the Arab world and the revival of past Arab glory. Others, which flourished especially during the fourth and fifth decades of the present century, betrayed Nazi and Fascist influences which still cling to the political thinking of some Arab youth and nationalist leaders, even after the destruction of the leading Nazi and Fascist states in Europe.

There are also many "progressive" movements which range from moderate traditional socialism to extreme Marxist socialism. The moderate socialists subordinate socialist theory to nationalist concepts and impregnate it with nationalist Arab traditions. The Marxists aim at creating a new Arab nationalism, nationalism as national in form but international Marxist in content. Some nationalist movements, particularly the "progressive," have taken a definite stand toward Islam. They have clearly stated their determination to be independent of Islam in everything which pertains to the organization of the state, society, and public economy. The other movements, however, remain vague and equivocal toward Islam, primarily because the concepts of nationalism itself are still not clear in the minds of the leaders, who do not fully distinguish nationalism and Islamism, and also because the general public is strongly Islamic. Consequently all the Arab states except Lebanon, in spite of the modern foundation of most of them, announce in their various constitutions that the religion of the state, in principle at least, is Islam.

The Islamic political movements consider the Moslems of all races, languages, and homelands as one nation indivisible, and seek to unite them in one great Islamic state, or one tightly knit Islamic commonwealth. Islam, according to these movements, is the only fatherland which unites them and the only flag which commands their loyalty. They therefore seek to establish their state, with all its social, economic, and political systems, on foundations drawn from the teachings of Islam.[15] This ultimate aim of current Moslem political movements is the basis for the difference between them and the national movements in general. Furthermore, this aim arouses the fears of non-Moslem Arab communities and drives them to champion uncompromising local nationalist movements, or movements generally opposed to Arabism and Islam. It is the cause of the fears of Lebanese Christian groups, and the reason for their extreme separatism and their insistence upon the complete independence of Lebanon from the other Arab countries. The Lebanese Christian who, through Lebanese independence, has come to enjoy the dignity of a citizen, fears lest a state based on Islamic principles, should, in spite of tolerance and justice, consider him nothing more than a *dhimmi,* not entitled to enjoy all the rights due to the Moslem citizen.

These Moslem movements, too, arouse the apprehensions of many political leaders and educated men who believe in modern civilization and seek to build the new Arab social order upon its foundations. They are most anxious to preserve all the modern economic, political, intellectual, and social elements which have entered Arab life. They are convinced that Islam, though it has played in the past an important role in leading the Arabs to accomplishment and glory, would not offer a suitable foundation for Arab life either now or in the future.

Shortly after the Egyptian coup d'etat of 1952, a rumor swept the country that the Azhar University had submitted to the military government the draft of several edicts and regulations which would secure the establishment of Islamic government in the land. The news produced serious repercussions and confusion both in Egypt and outside. Some were jubilant, but others shuddered with fear and promptly denounced the alleged action of the Azhar. The reaction was so violent that the government found it necessary to issue a statement signed by General Najib himself dismissing the whole matter as a vicious hoax designed to confuse the public and cause dissension. The Shaykh al-Azhar followed with a declaration that "the Azhar submitted no such draft to the government," while the Minister of Pious Foundations *(awqaf),* Shaykh Ahmad Hasan al-Baquri, strongly criticized the rumor-mongers, and pointed out that the prerequisites for the Islamic state do not at present exist.[16]

In spite of the fact that the Islamic movements disagree with the Arab movements on long-range aims, there is agreement on immediate aims. The most serious and urgent of these immediate aims is the liberation of the Arab countries from colonialism and from all foreign manipulation. This aim is basic for the solution of all Arab problems, in the eyes of both Arab and Islamic movements, and must stand first. The second of these agreed aims is the unification of all Arab countries and the co-ordination of their economic resources for the general welfare of all. Both Islamic and Arab movements seek to bring about complete Arab unity, or at least a strong Arab federation. In the memorandum which the Ikhwan al-Muslimun submitted to the Egyptian government,[17] one reads the following, "The Ikhwan al-Muslimun is a catholic Islamic society committed to the task of realizing the aims for which Islam was revealed. . . as well as developing the national wealth, raising the standard of living, accomplishing social justice, extending social security to every citizen, taking part in social service, combatting ignorance, disease, poverty, and vice, and promoting charity. . . . Furthermore, the Ikhwan strive for the liberation of the Nile Valley, the Arab world, and the Islamic fatherland in its entirety from foreign domination, the aid of Moslem minorities in every land, the complete support of Arab unity, and the forward march towards Pan-Islamic Union."[18]

The Islamic movements advocate and work for the liberation of the Arab countries and for Arab unity because they consider the Arab world a part of the Islamic fatherland, and because they see in the liberation and unity of the Arab world a forward step towards the liberation of the Islamic fatherland and the formation of the desired Pan-Islamic Union. In the words of Sayyid Qutb, one of the more prominent and responsible representatives of the Islamic idea, "Colonialism is crushing us with its weight so that we can hardly breathe. Duty requires that we direct all our active efforts towards resistance—open resistance to colonialism, and ideological resistance to the people's democracies. The flag which unites us in this resistance [to East and West alike] is that of Islam. Some of us prefer to unite under the Arab flag. I would not oppose this, provided that this were temporary, aiming at a greater union [under the banner of Islam]. Indeed, there is no serious contradiction between Arab nationalism and Islamic nationalism if the former were conceived as a step along the way [to the latter]. The Arab fatherland is but a part of the Islamic fatherland. If we should liberate the Arab we would have liberated a part of the Islamic, with which we would seek to liberate the rest. The important thing for us today is to get together and co-operate just as the 'free world' co-operates against us. Every small country cannot, by itself alone, face an entire world. The short-sighted policy which limits us within our artificial geographical boundaries is folly itself. It is our duty at least to get together in accordance with the logic of the times, if not in accordance with the logic of Islam."[19]

Whither, then, the Arab world? Is it heading toward a national order which would retain the enduring and salutary in Arab civilization and culture and would adopt the good from the modern, regulating the life of the individual and society in accordance with science and equity, separating state from religion, and according all individuals freedom to worship as they wish? Or is it moving toward an Islamic theocratic state which would enforce all the teachings of Islam and all its precepts? It would seem that the Arabs have already made their choice. They have already made some strides, long in some Arab countries, short in others, along the road towards the national order, as opposed to the theocratic state. It would seem that they are determined to continue along this road, the road of civilized nations in these modern times, to the end. Western civilization and culture have made very deep inroads in the Arab world. Indeed, the Arab world has set its face towards the West, and has made up its mind to acquire and use the material civilization of the West, together with its economic, political, and social systems. Moslem Arabs have accepted these things, perhaps a little reluctantly and with a measure of apprehension at the beginning. They have, however, got accustomed to them and have come to realize their benefits, with the result that they have now accepted them and are constantly seeking more of them.

People no longer argue concerning the benefits of the machine, artificial fertilizers, the use of quinine against malaria, the automobile and the railway, economic organization, commercial companies and banks, or the use of modern weapons instead of swords and scimitars. They no longer inquire whether the natural sciences and their technological applications involve belief or unbelief. Nor do they any longer question many innovations in politics, economics, and sociology which confront them wherever they turn. All these have become actualities in their world, indispensable to their everyday life.

Nor do people disagree any more concerning the material bases of Western civilization, and concerning the theoretical and experimental sciences upon which it rests. They may disagree on the moral foundations of this civilization, and in this they are not alone. The West itself has argued and disagreed and continues to argue and to disagree respecting these moral foundations, and expends much effort to evolve means of building society upon firmer foundations of justice and morality. In fact, the various communist, socialist, Fascist, and

156

Nazi movements, and the various Christian reform movements were to some extent the result of grave doubts concerning the moral foundations upon which Western civilization rests.

The Arab world has chosen to march along the path of that civilization which people call Western civilization. It is, however, a well-nigh universal civilization, which has drawn upon many civilizations, including the Arab and Islamic. It has been and is still being enriched by orientals and occidentals, believers and unbelievers alike. The Arab world has no intention of turning its back upon this civilization. Consequently the efforts of those investigators and scholars from both the East and the West who occupy their time and that of their readers with the study of the attitude of Islam towards Western civilization are sheer waste, and savour more of artless naïveté than of serious study. The Moslem Arabs have accepted this civilization, and are regulating, or endeavoring to regulate, their life in accordance with the sciences and ideas which it has developed. They are striving to enrich their existence with the material benefits it has produced, never inquiring whether or not in so doing they are acting in agreement or in disagreement with Islam. Underlying these material means of industry and art are the theoretical and the experimental sciences. The material means cannot be had without acceptance of the theoretical basis. This the Arabs know, and accept as a logical conclusion.

XI. Disparity in Political Development

It has already been pointed out that the Arab countries differ from one another considerably in sovereignty, form of government, and administrative organization. Some are "independent," like Iraq, Syria, Lebanon, the Hashimite Kingdom of Jordan, the Kingdom of Saudi Arabia, Yemen, Egypt, and the United Kingdom of Libya. Others are officially British protectorates but in actual practice subject to British domination, like Kuwait, Bahrein, Qatar, the Sheikhdoms of the Trucial Coast, the Sultanate of Muscat and Oman, and

Aden Protectorate (Hadramaut). Tunisia and Morocco are subject to French protection, or to direct French rule—which amount to the same thing in practice. Spanish Morocco is officially and actually subject to Spanish rule, while Tangier is an international zone, administered by several powers, with Spain enjoying the leading role in practice. Aden is a crown colony, linked directly with the British Crown, while Algeria officially forms a part of metropolitan France. The Sudan has been since 1899 a condominium administered by Britain and Egypt; but in practice, especially since the assassination of the Sirdar Sir Lee Stack on November 19, 1924, the Sudan has been administered by Britain alone almost as a colony.* Alexandretta has been ceded to Turkey, and Arabistan forms officially a part of Iran. Finally there is Palestine, partitioned by the United Nations and occupied by the Zionists, while the majority of its indigenous Arab inhabitants are now homeless refugees.

The majority of the Arab countries enjoy no national sovereignty at all, but are subject to foreign rule which controls their fate and future. Even those Arab countries listed as "independent" do not enjoy the complete national sovereignty of countries which are really independent. Iraq and Jordan have been bound to Britain by dictated treaties which vitiate their national sovereignty and leave Britain free to use their territories and ports as bases for its air, land, and sea forces in times of peace and war.[1] In Iraq, Britain has two large bases for its air force: al-Shu'aybah and al-Habbaniyyah. Britain also has absolute control over the Port of Basrah, the great sea base on the Persian Gulf. In Jordan, Britain has several air bases and the Arab Legion itself. British troops are still in the Suez Canal Zone.† So far as British influence is concerned, Libya is very much like Jordan, although French in-

---

* See p. 98, note 11. The elections of the fall of 1953, carried out in accordance with the terms of the agreement between the government of General Mohammed Najib of Egypt and the British government, resulted in the victory of the anti-British parties. The future of the Sudan, however, is far from settled.

† On October 19, 1954, Egypt's seventy-two-year struggle to free itself from British occupation came to an end through the signing of an agreement between the two governments, by which British forces will be completely withdrawn from Egyptian territory within a period of twenty months from the date of the agreement.

fluence competes with that of the British in certain parts, while the United States has control over the airports and seaports. Vestiges of Italian influence over its economy are still discernible. For the maintenance of the growing economic interests, particularly in petroleum, of the Western powers, for the safeguard of Israel's international existence, and for the use of the Arab countries' strategic position in their various political and military plans, these powers—Britain, France, Spain, and even the United States—miss no opportunity to intervene in the affairs of the Arab countries, both those which are technically independent and those which are not. Mention has already been made of the rivalries which exist among these powers, and the efforts which they have exerted to hinder any genuine *rapprochement* or co-operation of Arab states and other entities. It is obvious, therefore, that no sound Arab co-operation, front, or unity is possible until the Arab countries become fully independent and sovereign, free to administer their own affairs, determine their own fate, and choose the type of life agreeable to them.

As to the form of government, some Arab countries are nominally theocratic but actually autocratic, like Yemen and Saudi Arabia, where absolute individual rule prevails. Others are constitutional monarchies, like Jordan, Iraq, and Libya.*

* Until July, 1952, Egypt was supposed to be a constitutional monarchy. With the forced abdication of Faruq, a council of regency was formed to rule in the name of the infant Fuad II. On March 24, 1953, a subcommittee of the Constitution Committee recommended that Egypt should have a republican form of government. On June 18, the Military Council of the Revolution announced that the Egyptian monarchy had been brought to an end and proclaimed General Mohammed Najib as President and Prime Minister. The Council characterized its rule as transitional, leading eventually to the restoration of parliamentary government and the election of the President by the people. The period of transition was set at three years. Serious disagreement ensued on this very point between General Najib and Colonel Jamal 'Abd-al-Nasir, the real architect of the Revolution. Najib favored a speedier return to constitutional rule, while Nasir favored the continuation of military government. There followed the sudden ouster of Najib on February 25, 1954, his sudden restoration to the Presidency on February 27, and to the Premiership on March 8. The controversy continued through March and early April, when it was announced that the restoration of constitutional life to Egypt must be indefinitely deferred. On April 18, President Najib relinquished the Premiership to Colonel Nasir. On November 14, 1954, Najib's anomalous position was finally terminated when he was relieved of the Presidency as well. The immediate occasion was the uncovering of the Moslem Brotherhood's conspiracy to seize power, in which Najib is alleged to have had a part.

159

Others are democratic republics, like Syria and Lebanon. Still others are emirates and sheikhdoms, the internal affairs of which are administered in accordance with tribal custom and practice, like the Sheikhdoms of the Trucial Coast which stretch along the coast of the Persian Gulf and the Arabian Sea. In the Arab countries subject to foreign rule, government is in the hands of foreigners. They describe it as modern and democratic, but it is in reality arbitrary, enforced without the consent of the ruled.

In the "independent" Arab countries, the form of government is either democratic, at least in theory, or theocratic. The latter is exemplified in Yemen and Saudi Arabia. The fact of the matter, however, is that the Arab countries have known nothing of democracy except the name. Democratic government throughout the Arab world is going through a complex crisis and numerous tribulations, the most serious of which is that many educated Arabs and political leaders have come to doubt the soundness of the principles upon which Western democracy rests, and the possibility of applying its system in the Arab world. The underlying reasons for this crisis are, on the one hand, the ubiquitous foreign influence in the Arab world, and on the other the fact that those who introduced the democratic system of government into the Arab countries did not sincerely believe in it themselves. They did not therefore prepare a sound foundation for it among the people before they superimposed this new Western system upon these countries.

In the West, the democratic system of government grew as a result of a long struggle lasting for centuries between the rulers and the ruled. Democracy did not become firmly established until after the power of the feudal lords had been destroyed, feudalism itself abolished, Renaissance and later absolutisms replaced by increasingly representative systems, education spread among the people, and the right of the people established to express their views freely and to organize in political parties and labor unions without fear. Democratic government would remain weak and nominal unless it should

160

be supported by an educated general public free to express its views, at liberty to will and to do without coercion, to lead a life of sufficiency free from fear and assured of the safety of life, possessions, and source of livelihood.

But the colonial and Mandate powers which introduced the democratic type of government into the Arab world, and the ruling Arab dynasties which adopted it, did not think of raising it on sound and firm foundations. As a matter of fact they were not interested in establishing sound government which would serve the interests of the people and promote their progress. Rather they were concerned with beguiling the ruled into a belief that they were masters of their own government, and beguiling the civilized people who were involved in Arab affairs into believing that the governments in power were striving to educate those backward Arab peoples along the paths of progress, good government, and modern civilization. The occupying and Mandate powers and the ruling Arab dynasties strengthened feudalism, tribalism, and sectarianism, extended the influence of wealthy men and religious leaders, and spent the budgets of the various Arab countries on police and mercenary troops and on nonessentials, instead of spending them on educating the public, improving its health, and raising the standard of its living. The majority of the Arab public remains illiterate, ridden with poverty and disease, given to superstition, and resigned to the cunning of politicians. Arab peoples suffer from forgeries and falsifications in elections, intimidation of voters, and physical injury to their lives and property. They have not yet known a parliament which could bring about the fall of a corrupt cabinet by withholding confidence, or one which would watch over the public interest and the rights of the citizen. The absence of a sound democratic system of government, the weakness of the foundations of government, and constant foreign intervention, overt and covert, have transformed what was supposed to be democratic government in the Arab world into autocracies, or into rule by groups of wealthy and influential families, and have removed the people from active participa-

161

tion in political life. As a result of this lack of a truly democratic system, of the absence of constitutional rights and liberties, there has been much grumbling and popular dissatisfaction, and some of the Arab countries have been exposed to violent political disturbances. Perhaps the most serious of these have been those military coups d'etat in several Arab countries that resulted in the abrogation of all vestiges of democratic usage in constitutions, political parties, labor organizations, and organs of the press. The justification offered has always been the deterioration of the democratic system, the collapse of its foundations, and the corruption of its administrators. The military juntas which have seized power naturally declare that they are preparing the country for a better government and training the people for a future in which they will exercise their rights in a more truly democratic fashion—as though it were in the nature of military dictatorships to train people for sound democratic government.

The system of government that prevails in the Arab world rests on the arbitrary monopoly of political power by the few, while the people are kept from actively participating in the direction of public affairs. Such monopolies, and the diversity of forms of government, are obstacles to any unified Arab front. The conflicting interests of foreign countries in the Arab world, and the rivalries among ruling dynasties, are additional reasons for the weakening of the Arab front.

XII. Economic and Social Disparity

THE ARAB COUNTRIES suffer in varying degrees from economic and social disparity. Some still employ the ancient methods in agriculture and industry, while others, like Egypt, Lebanon, Syria, Iraq, and North Africa, have adopted modern means of farming and have introduced machinery into their agricultural production, although its use remains rather limited. The same is true of industry. Some countries—Egypt, Syria, Lebanon, and Iraq—have already begun to use modern means of manufacture. The other countries, however, remain without modern industries, especially big industries, and have therefore to depend on imported goods for meeting their needs, or on primitive handmade articles of local manufacture.

Similarly, the Arab countries suffer from disparity in the extent of their commercial progress and activity. Egypt, Syria, and Lebanon have made vast strides in commerce, to a point where they have become depots for supplying the other Arab countries with their own locally manufactured goods and with goods imported from foreign markets. In the other countries, commerce remains local in scope and backward in methods. With the disparity in the sources of natural wealth, in the fertility of the land, in the abundance of water, and in the density of population—with some countries overcrowded and others too thinly populated—there are marked disparities in the standard of living. The average income of the individual Arab remains greatly depressed in comparison with the average income of the individual in most countries of the civilized world. These factors have also produced a disparity in the mode of living. In some Arab countries tribal nomadic life still prevails, while in others life is geared to agriculture. Few have so far witnessed the growth of a large capitalist class, industrial and commercial.

Perhaps the most serious factor in destroying the economic unity of the Arab countries is their political division. This division has produced insurmountable economic barriers. Every Arab country has its own customs barriers, currency, taxation, import and export laws, and laws regulating the transfer of capital and the movement of nationals. These economic boundaries, which rise high on top of artificial political boundaries, were completely unknown when most of the Arab countries were a part of the Ottoman empire. They were created by the colonial powers which apportioned the Arab world among themselves, and have been sustained and perpetuated by the industrial and commercial class which has since developed in the area and which derives from these economic barriers great benefits in augmenting its wealth and extending its interests. As a result of this economic division, Arab markets have shrunk, commercial rivalries have sprung up, and regional specialization in production has completely disappeared. Long-range and comprehensive plans for economic development have been rendered extremely difficult in an age when most countries are endeavoring to pursue comprehensive economic planning.

The Arab world has vast economic potentialities. Its fertile arable lands would be sufficient to maintain several times the number of its present population at a much higher standard of living if they were exploited scientifically and if they were more equitably distributed among the population. Its surface and underground water supplies could be made to irrigate all of its arable areas and generate all the necessary electric power if they were scientifically exploited. Its petroleum resources are great enough to support large industries, supplying them with power on the one hand and with the necessary capital on the other. As a matter of fact, the disparity of the Arab countries in natural resources and in economic capacities demands economic co-operation instead of competition and rivalry. Variations in natural resources and economic capacities call for regional specialization in industrial and agricultural production and in commercial services. Such specialization in production would save enormous efforts and expense, would improve quality, and would diminish harmful commercial competition. Economic co-operation would enable the Arab countries to become more nearly self-sufficient, since the products of one would complement the products of others in meeting the needs of the population, and would put port facilities and roads at the service of all. Complete economic unity, or at least customs union, would lead to the enlargement of the Arab market—one of the most important factors in the rise of big industries in the area. A large market would absorb the products of such an industry, reduce the cost of production, and so enable Arab industry to counteract the present foreign domination of markets. Industrialization is indispensable for the progress and growth of the Arab world. It is the means of conquering the poverty which breaks the back of its masses, and of solving the problem of its ever increasing population. But industrialization is impossible without a large and extensive market. Division of labor, which is one of the basic requisites of industrialization, depends essentially on an enlarged market. At present some of the Arab countries which have just entered the stage of industrialization have found it expedient to erect economic barriers between themselves and the other Arab countries in order to protect their developing industries, but they will soon find themselves compelled to level these barriers in order to win the vast Arab market, and in order to secure the enormous capital funds which are required by many modern industries, and which in many instances cannot be raised within single countries as they are now constituted.

The Arab world is in general agricultural. Agriculture is the backbone of its economy and, as it were, its principal industry, since the Arabs depend directly and indirectly mainly on the produce of the land. But agriculture in the Arab world still uses the ancient methods, and the prevailing system of land tenure is mainly feudal. This system requires a large landless class, which leads a life of misery, disease, poverty, and ignorance, while a few landlords flourish at the expense of the many. At the same time governmental financial legislation falls most heavily on the laboring classes, since most of the income of the state comes from indirect taxation which is ultimately paid by the poor. This feudal system is one of the most important factors depressing the level of production, individual and public, and thus restricting the national income.

The factors which exhaust land productivity and shrink crops are many. The most important are antiquated methods of agriculture, inadequate conservation and control of water resources, the poor care the peasant gives to his land because the feudal landlord robs him of the greater part of his crop, and the poor agricultural qualifications of the peasant himself. The feudal system is among the factors which have produced the existing disparities in the Arab world. The low purchasing power of Arab peasants, who form the overwhelming majority of the population, hinders the growth of big industries in the Arab world, and in turn prevents the development of commerce among its various countries. This feudal system also keeps most peasants from active participation in government, and from giving any serious thought to the fate of their country, and still less to the fate of the Arab world as a whole. It paralyzes the overwhelming majority of the nation in the field of national endeavor. As already stated, "nationalism" does not flourish solely as a result of a common language, history, traditions, and fatherland. Side by side with these there must exist a common will to life emanating from the consciousness of individuals, and an awareness of a common fate, dominating their thinking and impelling them to concerted action to bring the national life from the realm of the potential to the realm of the actual. The Arab peasant cannot rise to this national consciousness so long as he remains in the shadows of the feudal system, denied any education, surrounded with superstitions, isolated and insulated from the world outside, forced to sacrifice his human dignity for a crumb of bread, and driven by his leaders like a beast of burden possessing no will, or freedom, or mind.

In certain Arab countries, including Iraq, Jordan, Syria, Morocco, and Libya, nomadic Bedouins form an important part of the population, and in Saudi Arabia they constitute the overwhelming majority. The tribal system under which they live is even more detrimental than the feudal system to economic progress, the development of national consciousness, and the formation in the Arab world of a unified public opinion which might compel the rulers to work for the general Arab good. As producers, the Bedouins play a very insignificant role in the national economy. Even the cattle they raise fall short of the present requirements in both quality and number, because of the failure to employ scientific methods in feeding and breeding. As consumers, the Bedouins benefit the national economy very little because of the meagerness of their resources and the primitive simplicity of their life, the needs of which can be met with small quantities of the cheapest goods. Furthermore, the Bedouin's horizon is lim-

ited to his tribe. He knows no fatherland and cannot tolerate
the restraints of a modern state. He is not concerned whether
he be an Iraqi, a Syrian, or a Nejdite. Nor is he bothered by
the fact that his ruler may be a king, a dictator, or the president of a democratic republic. What concerns him is fertile
land where he can turn his cattle and camels to pasture. Which
state may hold the land is no concern of his. He understands
no official boundaries and recognizes no colored maps.

Upon the soil of feudalism and tribalism, autocratic rule
is established and the influence of ruling dynasties is reinforced. And upon this same soil the foundations of democracy
have given way and its edifice has collapsed.

XIII. Cultural Disparity

CULTURALLY THE ARAB countries greatly differ one from the
other. Some, like Syria, Lebanon, Iraq, Egypt, and Jordan,
have made marked cultural progress. The number of their
educated men and women is constantly increasing. Their
schools, colleges, and universities are flourishing. Private and
public libraries are rising in their towns and cities, and people
in general are reading more and better books than ever before.
On the other hand, most of the remaining Arab countries remain culturally retarded and their people for the most part
illiterate and ignorant. This cultural disparity is evident not
only between one Arab country and another, but also between
various parts of the same country. While cultural progress has
been marked in towns and cities, the larger cities in particular,
the countryside has generally remained far behind. Besides
the disparity in the spread of education, there is disparity in
the kind of education the student receives, in the methods employed for imparting it, in the sources of its support, and in the
schools themselves. They may be national or foreign, and in
either case sectarian or nonsectarian. University education is
divided by the rivalry of three different systems of education,
the French, the British, and the American, all superimposed
on the remnants of the Ottoman. Each has its own devotees

and followers, but for the most part university education in the Arab world is a hodgepodge of all three.[1]

Arab educators have long recognized the situation, and have repeatedly called for uniformity in education in the Arab world. In spite of the numerous inter-Arab conferences and in spite of the establishment within the League of Arab States of a special permanent committee for cultural affairs, little has been accomplished. It seems unlikely that the Arabs can make any progress toward uniformity so long as most of the Arab countries remain directly and indirectly subject to the domination of several foreign powers, each one of which is bent upon steering the educational and cultural policies of the country under its control in a direction which will safeguard its colonial interests and consolidate its influence. Furthermore, the Arab states have so far shown themselves incapable of agreement on almost every vital problem, not excluding the educational and the cultural.

The cultural problem is one of the major problems which confront the Arab world today. Essentially, however, it is not a problem of differences in educational systems, methods, and aims, but rather of the absence of any large degree of culture in the Arab world. In a civilized world in which the dominating powers employ science to control the weak, the Arab countries, which are far behind those powers in material civilization and culture, can hardly expect to achieve any liberation, unity, or progress without first educating their masses. Nor can the individual Arab, who remains for the most part illiterate and ignorant, have much sense of his own dignity or the dignity of his dismembered and oppressed fatherland.

The cultural famine which ravages Arab life is indeed not novel, nor is it the handiwork of colonial rule, feudal rapacity, and local oppression alone. As a matter of fact its roots go far back into the history of the Arab people. For Arab masses have from the beginning been illiterate and ignorant. Those to whom their affairs and destinies have been entrusted in recent times could and should have been able to solve the problem, or at least the major part of it. The masses in

Europe and the United States were not literate and educated a century or two ago. Today, however, relatively few illiterate adults exist in those lands. On the other hand, the colonial powers which spread their control over most of the Arab world, often on the pretext of educating and civilizing its people and preparing them for self-government, have done very little to better the educational and cultural conditions of their wards. In fact, in this as in almost everything else, colonialism's sins of omission have been far more serious than those of commission. The masses in the coastlands of the Peninsula and in the Sudan remain today, as they were when British control was extended over their countries, illiterate and ignorant. In North Africa, France paid its entire attention to the education of the *colons* and their offspring, but left the Arab masses almost without education. Furthermore, it sought to inculcate a disdain for Arab history in those North African students who had the opportunity to attend government schools.[2]

On the other hand, the progress made by independent Arab countries in the field of education has been notable, especially since the end of the First World War. In 1920-1921, Iraq, for example, had 88 primary schools for both boys and girls, with 486 teachers and 7,452 students.[3] In 1950-51, the number stood at 1,479 primary and secondary schools (private and governmental) with 9,196 men and women teachers and 243,279 students of both sexes.[4] Even greater progress has been accomplished in Lebanon, Syria, Egypt, and Jordan. Marked as this progress may seem, it is nevertheless slow and insufficient in relation to the needs of the various Arab countries and their economic and human resources, and in view of the favorable conditions of modern times. Too many children of school age can still find no place at all in school. Among the causes for this slow progress is the failure of the Arab governments to give education, particularly in the countryside, the necessary attention. Education claims only 10 per cent of the national budget.[5] The problem is not limited to the education of the school-age generation but extends to the education of illiterate adults. As yet the efforts of Arab governments in fighting illiteracy have been superficial and inadequate.

The educational problem in the Arab world is organically linked with its other problems, the economic, the social, and the political, and cannot be solved unless they are also solved. Thus as a result of the prevailing system of land tenure and the antiquated methods of agriculture, the Arab peasant remains generally poor, and is impelled to press his children into farm labor or herding instead of sending them to school. As a tenant farmer, he is at the mercy of the landlord. Consequently he is a continual state of instability, moving from one farm to another, and from one village to another. This constant instability has been one of the major causes for the failure of village education. Furthermore, the feudal landlords often obstruct or prevent the establishment of schools in their villages, because they realize that the exploitation and control of an educated farm worker are more difficult than the exploitation and the control of the uneducated, and because they also realize that schools would rob them of abundant and therefore cheap farm labor. And to what end would the peasant put his education? His village is devoid of cultural clubs and libraries. Nor are there any mobile library services which could supply him with books, magazines, or newspapers. Actually, neither education in particular nor culture in general has yet become an obvious need for the peasant. Until he is made to see the need, he is not likely to bestir himself to acquire them, still less to see any benefit in sending his children to school.

The same is true of the problems of illiteracy, which is closely linked to the economic and social conditions of the Arab world, and which cannot be finally overcome until there is change and improvement in these spheres. For a higher general level of culture and education will not be achieved unless a certain measure of leisure and material well-being exists. So long as farm workers and laborers remain desperately poor, forced to toil all day with primitive tools in order to insure their equally primitive livelihood, they are unlikely to realize the benefits of education or to bother about getting it. Nor could they under present conditions find any time for learning even if the urge should be present. How can the nomad Bedouin in his constant movement with his flocks in search of pasture and a waterhole seek and acquire an education? Or how can the poverty-ridden, illiterate "man with the hoe" perceive the need for learning in an environment in which he never sees a book? These people have grown up in illiteracy and ignorance, and naturally have no remorse for not having sought what they never knew. To change the deplorable economic condition of the majority of the people would not only raise their standard of living, promote their social stability, increase their feeling of security, and add to their leisure, but would also bring about a general change in their mentality, enkindle hope in their minds, give them self-confidence, imbue them with the dignity of free men and women, and make them more prepared to seek education and to enrich their lives with its benefits.

This dark picture has tended to make reformers stand still, passively awaiting rectification of economic conditions before beginning to fight illiteracy and promote learning. Few of these reformers realize that as the reorganization of economic life would facilitate the solution of the problem of illiteracy, the education of the masses would basically help in the betterment of social and economic conditions. They still have to learn that organized efforts to eradicate illiteracy should go side by side with efforts to raise the standards of living generally. This will require careful planning, qualified teachers, suitable books, and proper facilities capable of attracting the tired laborer and the exhausted farm worker. Obviously such an undertaking calls for enormous sums of money and a government profoundly conscious of the need for educating the masses. Financial problems, those of administrative organization in existing governments and those of the relations between rulers and the ruled, will arise, and must be faced, as soon as realistic attempts to deal with the problem are made.

171

From the beginning educational policies in the Arab world had the wrong orientation. Arab governments were interested in training civil servants, and educated persons were interested in becoming government officials. Government service, therefore, became the life aim of the educated. Failure to secure a governmental job, no matter how lowly, meant that they went unemployed. With government bureaus full to capacity, the educated for whom there is no place have reached dangerous numbers. The situation is becoming increasingly serious from day to day. Yet the need of the Arab world today is for trained technicians and experts in industry and agriculture.

Arab societies still neglect the woman, leaving her illiterate, ignorant, and ignored, allowed no share in the economic, political, and constructive life of her country, although she is half the social order and the mother of future generations.* The position of woman in society is one of the best standards for measuring the cultural development of that society. The extent to which she is progressive and free is the index to the progress of that society. No wonder that the Arab world remains backward, tradition-fettered, and limping behind the procession of human achievement, when woman's status is so low![6] If Arab woman is to be freed from the impediments to her creative vitality, the Arab man must be first freed from those oppressive economic conditions which paralyze the will, disfigure life, and poison the spirit. When man becomes educated and his soul is refined by culture, the day of liberation for the woman will arrive.

The problem of education and formal schooling has been discussed, but the attainment of a general level of education among the public does not depend on schools alone. Its wider media include the press, the book, the radio, the cinema, and all social, political, and cultural societies. Prevailing economic conditions, social conditions, and particularly political conditions, help to smother education by these media. The press is subject to many harsh curbs which restrict its freedom, limit

---

* It must be noted in this connection that literate women have been enfranchised in Syria in 1949 and in Lebanon in 1953.

172

its horizons, and reduce it to the position of a lackey to government. It has been plagued by regulations which destroy its freedom, by censorship, by martial law and proclamations of a state of siege, imposed by rulers for reason and for no reason.* In such an atmosphere only a mercenary press which flatters rulers and misguides the public, diverting it from its own agonies and from the country's misfortunes, can flourish. The Arab radio is government-owned and -directed, serving its will and purpose. As to the Arab cinema, the concern of its owners is quick wealth at the expense of morality and good taste.

The problem of the Arabic book—the free book which renders its service of criticism, reform, guidance, and enlightenment—is today the problem of Arab thought in general. And the problem of Arab thought is the problem of freedom —freedom of thought and freedom of expression. In spite of the various features of material progress in the means of writing, printing, publishing, and promotion, the Arabic book is still exposed to the danger of confiscation if it does not toe the official line. It cannot easily deviate from what is laid down by the fanaticism of religious leaders, the caprice of local despots, and the time-honored traditions of the general public. Religious leaders of all faiths fear the free book, not because it might conceivably constitute a threat to their scriptures, but because it might endanger their power, which rests in most cases on ignorance and obscurantism. Local despots fear the book because their authority rests on force and coercion rather than on freedom and voluntary consent. The general public is ignorant, and is allowed no scope except to toy with its superstitions and hold fast to its worn-out traditions.

The struggle of the Arabic book is but a part of the struggle of defenseless right against armed oppression, of truth against falsehood, and of science against superstition. A book does not flourish except in wide horizons, and thought does

---

* At the time of writing, three large and independent Arab states, Iraq, Syria, and Egypt, were under military rule.

not prosper except in freedom. Only free men dare to think; and it is only through free thought, freely expressed, that the Arabic book can be kept alive, to fulfill its mission of reviving the spirit of freedom among the Arabs until they regain their place in history, and recapture the opportunity to participate, as free men and women, in its making.

The problem of the Arab world today is the problem of liberating most of its countries from foreign rule and domination, of delivering Palestine from Zionism, and of achieving economic, social and intellectual progress throughout its lands. It is the problem of regaining for the Arab individual his human dignity, and restoring to the Arab fatherland its international position and prestige. This can only be achieved by a people educated to realize itself, its problems, and the way for their solution. And between those in power, who strive to keep the Arab public illiterate and ignorant, and enlightened patriots, who labor to lead the people to liberty, light, and happiness, is a constant and fateful struggle. But survival is for the fittest always; and the future belongs to the forces of light among the children of life.

XIV. Conclusion

THE PRECEDING PAGES have shown that the problem of the Arab world today is threefold: liberating the Arab fatherland from foreign rule and domination in order to effect eventually some kind of unity; achieving economic, social, and cultural progress throughout its lands; and delivering Palestine from the Zionists. The three are interrelated. It has been seen how foreign rule and domination have obstructed unity, retarded progress beyond the minimum necessary for colonial interests, and established the state of Israel. Obviously, the solution is also interrelated. But of the three, the last is perhaps the most urgent. For Israel, as already stated, is the most serious danger to which the Arab world has been exposed since the period of the Crusaders. With outside support, official and private, Israel stands as a spear stuck into the heart of the Arab fatherland. Since its creation, Israeli plans have admittedly been to bring *all* Jews to Palestine,[1] and a stream of inflowing population has steadily poured into the country, making inevitable the eventual problem of living space. The Zionists' ultimate goal has often been stated as an Israel extending from the Euphrates to the Nile. Israel, too, is a veritable wedge which has split the Arab world in twain, separating the lands of the Fertile Crescent from the African Arabs in Egypt and beyond. With superior vitality, technical skill, and outside aid, Israel hopes to strangle budding Arab industries and to open the vast market to its own.

When viewed against the background of present Arab conditions and the current world situation, the rise of the state of Israel would be recognized as a factor tending to transform the Arab problem from one of liberation, unity, and progress to one of survival or extinction.[2] The division of the world into two contending camps and the vital interests of both in the Arab fatherland, at once for its *middle* position and its natural resources, make the Arab world an essential area in any future conflict. Arab survival, therefore is irrevocably linked with the larger world problem—that of peace or war. Yet the part which the Arabs can play in determining the course of events is small, and depends on the extent to which they can participate with other nations for the preservation of peace. Nor does Arab survival depend on any neutral position they might wish to take. Actually the choice is not theirs to make, because of the nature of the geographic and strategic location of their fatherland and also because of their obvious inability to maintain such a position, even if they so desire.

The problem of survival is equally present in the case of Israel. Unless it succeeds in becoming "levantinized," its future would in all likelihood be similar to that of the Latin Kingdom of Jerusalem in the twelfth century. As outside aid and support diminish and Arab unity and strength grow, Israel's zero hour would arrive and its final fate would be sealed. The story would then become another chapter in the long history of the Holy Land.

In the face of the present situation, therefore, the Arabs have but one course to follow, one principle on which to base all their policies and actions: the extent to which any policy or any action would mitigate, immediately or in the long run, the danger of Israel. This is the yardstick against which all Arab effort will be measured.

Notes

I. Arab and Arab World

1. In his pamphlet, *The Arabs,* Oxford, 1940, p. 3, H. A. R. Gibb states, "To the question 'Who are the Arabs?' there is—whatever ethnographers may say—only one answer which approaches historic truth: all those are Arabs for whom the central fact of history is the mission of Mohammed and the memory of the Arab Empire, and who in addition cherish the Arabic tongue and its cultural heritage as their common possession."

Bernard Lewis, *The Arabs in History,* London, 1951, p. 9, states, "A gathering of Arab leaders some years ago defined an Arab in these words: 'Whoever lives in our country, speaks our language, is brought up in our culture, and takes pride in our glory is one of us.' "

Sati' al-Husari, one of the earliest and most eminent leaders concerned with the Arab national problems, writing in *al-Hayat,* August 5, 1951, states: "The apparent differences among the populations of the Arab states are accidental and superficial, and do not justify the assumption that they are members of different nationalities, simply because they are citizens of different states, all of which have come into being as a result of the maneuvres and horse-trading tactics of the Powers. . . . There is no doubt whatsoever that Egypt is a part of the Arab world so long as it shares with all the other Arab countries the same language, culture, and long history, to say nothing of the afflictions and dangers it has in common with them. Furthermore, it is geographically linked to them directly, thereby becoming the heartland of the extensive Arab world. There are several Arab peoples, but all of them belong to one nation, the Arab nation. . . . Any member of these Arab peoples is an Arab."

W. B. Fisher, *The Middle East,* London, 1950, pp. 77-99, discussing the various races from whom the people of the Middle East are descended, states in summary (p. 91): ". . . We may say that from the point of view of the anthropologist, it is impossible to speak with any accuracy either of an Arab or of a Semitic people. Both terms connote a mixed population varying widely in physical character and in racial origin, and are best used purely as cultural and linguistic terms respectively."

See also George Antonius, *The Arab Awakening,* Philadelphia, 1939, pp. 13-19.

In tracing the development of the word "Arab" in history, Bernard Lewis (*The Arabs in History,* pp. 9-17) states that the word was for centuries before Islam used of the Bedouins. In Greco-Roman usage its meaning was extended to include the nomadic population of the Arabian Peninsula and those settled around the different oases, as well as the South Arabians. After the Moslem conquest it was applied to the conquerors to distinguish them from the people of the conquered territories. When the Arab Empire became a Moslem Empire, the word came to be employed to describe the various facets of the civilization of the Caliphate, which was produced by men of many nations and faiths, but which was Arabic in language and to a large extent in general character. Later, when the conquerors became assimilated in the people of the conquered territories, the term gradually lost its ethnic connotation and became in effect a social term, reverting to its earlier meaning of bedouin or nomad, while the Arabic-speaking townspeople and peasantry were called *abna' al-'arab* to distinguish them from the non-Arabic-speaking Moslems.

In conclusion, Lewis states (p. 17): "While all these different usages have survived in certain contexts to the present day, a new one born of the impact of the West has in the last fifty years become increasingly important. It is that which regards the Arabic-speaking peoples as a nation or group of sister nations in the European sense, united by a common territory, language and culture and a common aspiration to political independence."

The accepted criteria for an Arab, therefore, according to the preceding views, include a common territory, language, history, traditions, customs, culture, and society. The religious criterion, alluded to by Gibb, is considered by some, particularly those among whom religion still holds sway and national consciousness is still weak—as it is the case today in the Peninsula and North Africa—to be one of the principal bonds of unity. But because of the rapid spread of education, the trend is away from religion and race. Modern nationalist Arabs are as proud of the mission of Mohammed and of the glories of the Arab Empire as the conservative Moslems, but they look upon them as products of Arab genius and mentality.

2. The term Syria is used throughout this book for the territory now including the Republic of Syria, the Republic of the Lebanon, and the territory now forming Jordan and Israel, until recently known as Palestine and Transjordan.

3. See George Antonius, *The Arab Awakening*, Philadelphia, 1939, p. 17, n. 1, where Louis Massignon is quoted from *Revue du Monde Musulman*, LVII (1924) to the effect that "nearly two-thirds of the settled Moslem population of Palestine is of original Arab stock. In Transjordan the percentage is still higher."

II. Natural Divisions of the Arab World

1. Fisher, p. 446.
2. Fisher, p. 427.
3. Fisher, pp. 436-37.
4. Fisher, pp. 439-41.
5. Fisher, pp. 441-44.
6. Fisher, pp. 450-52.

III. Political Divisions of the Arab World

1. Accurate censuses for any part of the Arab world are simply not found. In this study, the most recent census and estimates have been utilized.

IV. Basic Unifying Factors

1. N. A. Faris, "The Case against the Colloquial," *The Moslem World*, XXXII, No. 4 (October, 1942), 329.

2. Annual celebration of Mohammed's birthday and the Moslem New Year by Moslems everywhere, celebration of the Day of 'Ashura,' particularly by the Shiites, who re-enact its tragic events, are all examples of the same phenomenon. For Shiite celebration of the Day of 'Ashura,' see Ernest Main, *Iraq—from Mandate to Independence*, London, 1933, pp. 158-61; see also Carleton S. Coon, *Caravan*, New York, 1952, p. 124.

3. See Ma'ruf al-Rusafi, *Nahnu w-al-Madi*, 3rd Edition, Cairo, 1931, pp. 34-36.

4. Arab mentality has been investigated by Isma'il Mazhar in his book, *Wathbat al-Sharq*, Cairo, 1929. A more penetrating study is that by Ali Wardi, entitled *Shakhsiyyat al-Fard al-'Iraqi*, Bagdad, 1951. Wardi's work, though devoted to the Iraqi individual, is true of the Arabs in general. He notes that the Iraqi mentality betrays a deep-rooted duality resulting from marginal life between nomadism and city life. The Iraqi individual has, therefore, two sets of values contending for his loyalty. One, which is nomadic and tribal, exalts courage and pride; the other, which is urban, stresses hardships and endurance, submission and cunning. This duality is further enhanced by a social order which segregates men and women, and by the type of education the individual receives in the home, school, and street, as well as by the difference which exists between classical Arabic, the literary instrument, and the colloquial tongue, for everyday purposes.

5. From remote times, the Arab world has been exposed to waves of raiders and conquerors. Since, for the most part, these conquerors used to descend upon the Arab world in numerical strength too small to give them control of all regions, they were content to occupy the settled centers and cities and to fasten their yoke upon the other parts, particularly the countrysides and villages, exacting from them excessive taxes and suppressing their public feeling. Consequently, there grew in the minds of the people in general, and among the peasantry in particular, hatred of all established authority, suspicion of all its representatives, and a belief that all governments are evil and their overthrow highly desirable whenever the opportunity should arise. The subjugation of the people by despotic governments, mostly foreign, inculcated among them fear of these governments, weakened their self-confidence, and destroyed their self-respect and personal dignity. This may explain the successive uprisings of the people against established government, uprisings which no sooner flare up than they subside, and soon are transformed to abject submission and whispered grumblings.

6. Ameen Rihani, *Muluk al-'Arab*, 3rd ed., Beirut, 1953, I, 117, relates the following conversation he had with one of his Yemenite escorts, a member of the *Sadah* class (nobility): "Smiling, Sayyid Muhammad said, . . . I will instruct you with something you know nothing about. You have complained that our homes are small and narrow, their ceilings low, and their windows very small. Were you to travel in 'Asir, you would find there the homes still smaller and darker. Do you know why this is so? The people of Yemen and 'Asir are still savage; not one of them would trust his brother. They live in perpetual fear and anxiety. This is the way they sleep in 'Asir'—saying this, he reached his rifle, held it to his side, and hugged it close to himself—'this is the way they sleep. They are like wild beasts which fear everything and everybody that may come near them. As to the Yemen, you have seen with your own eyes that all people are armed, all fight, and all kill for the least thing. We are very jealous of our rights. Holding with his hand a small coffee cup, he said, 'What is the value of this?' Hardly a thing, but it is mine; it is my property. If you should take it, you would have robbed me of my own property. You would not then hear me remonstrate or protest. No. I would fight you.' Brandishing a dagger held firmly to the side of his belt, he resumed his conversation and said, 'I will draw this dagger and kill you, I will cut your throat.' This is our way of life in Yemen. If in this village two houses should suddenly engage in a fight, the entire population would split into two parties and join in the fight. War would break out in the village. When it subsides, and only then, would the people ask what the cause of the fighting was. They first fight, and then inquire as to the cause of the fight. This is our way of life in Yemen. We fight our own relatives. The brother would fight his own brother, the son his own father. If this is the way we live among ourselves, how would you think we would live with strangers and foreigners?"

7. Antonius, p. 89.

V. New Unifying Factors

1. Given by the Vatican to the Lebanese monastery at Dayr Qazhayya. In Syria, Aleppo had the first printing press in 1698. These two were followed by one in Shwair, Lebanon, in 1732, and that of St. George's in 1753. In Egypt, the first Arabic printing press came with Napoleon in 1798, and was later installed in Bulaq in 1822. The American press was first founded in Malta in 1820, but in 1832 was moved to Beirut, where it still remains.

2. Such as Butrus al-Bustani, Nasif al-Yaziji and his son Ibrahim, Ahmad Faris al-Shidyaq, Adib Ishaq, 'Abd-al-Rahman al-Kawakibi, Ma'ruf al-Rusafi, Jamil Sidqi al-Zahawi, Shibli Shmayyil, Ya'qub Sarruf, Jurji Zaydan, and Ameen Rihani.

3. ". . . On the Persian Gulf, on the extreme east of the Arabian Peninsula, in al-Qatif, are active learned men and literators who look to Egypt, hail its name, and

179

applaud its contribution in the arts and the sciences. They are especially proud, as stated by Hasan ibn-'Ali abu-al-Su'ud, of the bonds of blood, language, and religion which exist between them. They esteem Egypt, and find in Egyptian culture a rich source of refreshment and light. The same idea was expressed by another learned man of al-Qatif, Muhammad Sa'id al-Shaykh al-Khunayzi, when he stressed the importance of the link of thought and spirit which binds the learned men of both, in spite of the vast deserts and seas which separate them." See Bint al-Shati', *Ard al-Mu'jizat,* Series *Iqra',* No. 104, Cairo, September, 1951, pp. 122-23.

4. A number of the leading actors and actresses in the Egyptian cinema are Lebanese or of Lebanese and Syrian descent.

5. Like the Istiqlal party and the Ba'th club in Iraq and 'Usbat al-'Amal al-Qawmi party in Lebanon. The last of these joined the Nida' party in 1952.

6. Like the National Democratic Party and the Nationalist Socialist Party in Iraq. For the position of the different Arab political parties in Syria, Lebanon, and Iraq regarding Arab nationalism and Arab political co-operation, see Sati' al-Husari, *al 'Urubah bayn Du'atiha wa-Mu'aridiha,* Beirut, 1952, pp. 149-81.

7. In an interview with the Iraqi newspaper, *Sada 'l-Ahali,* published on September 30, 1951, Mohammed ibn-'Allal al-Fasi, president of the Istiqlal (independence) Party of Morocco, said: "The Istiqlal Party of Morocco, which has led the Moroccan national movement ever since its inception, considers itself under an obligation not to betray the confidence placed in it by the various Arab agencies which have given it its full support throughout its most recent crisis. Consequently, it wishes to affirm that the goal for which it is striving, *after achieving the independence of Morocco,* is the fulfillment of the aspirations of Arab nationalists for freedom, unity, and social justice throughout the rest of the Arab world."

8. "Now that al-Damman, Dhahran, Hasa, al-Kharj, and al-Riyad have been linked by railroad, the Saudi authorities have laid down plans for a four-year project at the conclusion of which al-Riyad would be linked by railroad to al-Qusaym, Medina, Jedda, and Mecca" (*Al-Ruwwad,* Beirut, February, 21, 1952).

9. The President of the Beirut Chamber of Commerce and Industry declared at the Chambers of Commerce Conference, held in Beirut during January, 1951: "Co-operation among the Arab countries is no longer a hollow myth, but an actual reality. Arab economic circles realize that they possess interests each complementing the others. It is, therefore, natural that this situation should result in the growth of closer co-operation among them." See *Sada 'l-Ahali,* No. 674, Bagdad, January 18, 1951.

10. Ample evidence is available that the French Foreign Office gave financial aid to the University of St. Joseph prior to the establishment of the Mandate. During the period of the French Mandate, this University extended its influence over the systems of education in both Syria and Lebanon. Although both these Arab countries gained their "full" independence after the end of the Second World War and are at present members of the United Nations Organization, their systems of education are still dominated by French influence, overt and covert, and the University of St. Joseph is second only to the French political missions in maintaining that influence. In this connection it is not out of place to note that at the time the French were suppressing the Jesuit Order in Metropolitan France, they were subsidizing its activities in the Arab East.

The Syrian Protestant College, which became in 1920 the American University of Beirut, has a much cleaner record. The only time this institution received funds from governmental sources is when it accepted on behalf of the region Point IV money for the education of about 118 Arab students in accordance with programs approved by their own governments. Nevertheless, this action by the University drew censure from various circles, including some of its own faculty.

11. The American Mission was the first to prepare a modern Arabic translation of the Bible. Its feat induced the Jesuits to follow suit and to prepare a translation of their own.

12. See Sati' al-Husari, *Hawliyyat al-Thaqafah al-'Arabiyyah*, Cairo, 1950, pp. 9-16; Antonius, pp. 35-45.

13. *The Middle East*, pp. 75-77.

14. Both Britain and France, but particularly the latter, were trying during the years preceding the War to foment Arab feeling in Syria and the Lebanon against the Ottoman Empire.

15. The author should know, having played in it a very minor role, as Head of the Arabic Desk at the Office of War Information, Overseas Operation Branch, New York City.

16. No mention is made of the annual conferences which Arab lawyers, physicians, engineers, and educators hold, and of the profound influence they have in bringing the various Arab countries closer together, since these conferences do not fall within the scope of this chapter.

17. The events which preceded and succeeded the arbitrary overthrow and exile of the Sultan of Morocco, Sidi Mohammed bin Youssef, by the French in August, 1953, are such an example.

VI. Dynastic Rivalries

1. The word for nationalization in Arabic is *ta'mim*. It could also mean making anything the property of the Imam, the head of the theocratic state. When therefore Mossaddegh declared the petroleum industry of Iran nationalized, some talk of nationalizing the Saudi Arabian petroleum industry was heard. A wisecrack then asserted that it was already nationalized, being the property of the Imam.

2. When about a decade ago, the first Saudi Arabian budget was made, and the Minister of Finance hesitatingly and politely suggested that His Majesty was going beyond the budget, the Minister was kicked out of the royal presence with the remark, "Whose money do you think this is, thou son of the infidel woman?"

3. The regimes of Bisharah al-Khuri of Lebanon and Shukri al-Quwwatly in Syria are excellent examples.

4. Described by a British authority as "a monument of ambiguity." See Reader Bullard, *Britain and the Middle East*, London, 1951, p. 69.

5. Antonius, pp. 328-29.

6. In his *Muluk al-'Arab*, II, 63, Ameen Rihani relates that ibn-Saud had shown him a letter from King Husayn, the gist of which was as follows: "King Husayn calls upon the Sultan to conclude peace and to declare his loyalty to him [Husayn]." This invitation carried conditions, of which the most important were that Tarabah and al-Kharmah should be given back to the Hejaz and that ibn-al-Rashid should have his throne in Ha'il and his control over Jebel Shammar restored to him.

7. The Treaty of Mecca, dated January 22, 1926.

8. In his *Muluk al-'Arab*, vol. II, p. 61, Ameen Rihani quotes the following remonstrance by ibn-Saud, ". . . The British are indebted to us. This is the truth, Professor. Yet we do not demand of them anything. It would be a shame to demand anything. But what is their present policy? You see them scheme and scheme! You see them plot against me, ibn-Saud, their friend! They have surrounded me with enemies, and raised petty states round about me, and enthroned my enemies as kings to whom they always extend financial and political aid—the Sharif in the Hejaz, his son Abdullah in Transjordan, and his [other] son Faysal in Iraq. What is the purpose of these actions, and what calls for their doing? I, ibn-Saud, am the friend of the British, but through their sharifian policy, they treat me as they would treat an enemy! . . . And who is ibn-Saud to the Sharif and his sons? He is the crude unbe-

liever, the stiff-necked Kharijite. This is the truth, Professor. They have said that and even more. And yet they ask and expect me to attack the French in Syria to drive them out. This is the truth. . . ."

9. *Muluk al-'Arab*, I, 76.

10. *Ibid.*, II, 101-2.

11. Recent Saudi-Jordanian *rapprochement* is dictated by fear of possible Iraqi-Jordanian union and consequent loss of the Jordan throne to the Hashimite branch of Iraq. This fear is being exploited by both the Saudis and the Egyptians in order to forestall such union. It is therefore indicative of rivalry rather than amity.

12. Known henceforward as the National Congress (al-Mu'tamar al-Watani).

13. *Suriyya al-Kuba, The Jordanian White Paper*, Amman, n.d., pp. 5-9.

14. For the text of the political memorandum which the Emir Adbullah submitted, in 1943, to Mr. Richard Casey, British Minister of State in the Middle East, see *Suriyya al-Kubra, The Jordanian White Paper*, pp. 64-70. The memorandum contains the texts of both plans, the unified state and the federated state.

15. *Kalimat al-Suriyyin w-al-'Arab fi Mashru' Suriyyah al-Kubra*, 1st ed., September, 1947, pp. 60-61.

16. For the text of the statement of the League of Arab States, see *ibid.*, pp. 24-25.

17. *Al-Ahram*, Cairo, September 27, 1952.

18. By King Abdullah.

VII. THE FOREIGN POWERS

1. Quoted by Antonius, p. 31, from Sir Henry L. Bulwer's *Life of Palmerston*, II.

2. See *al-'Urubah bayn Du'atiha wa-Mu'aridiha*, pp. 12-15, where the causes for the creation of Transjordan and not for uniting it either with Iraq or Palestine are fully discussed.

3. The most illustrous case was the assassination of Lord Moyne, the British Minister Resident in the Middle East, on November 6, 1944, by two members of the Stern Group, in Cairo.

4. Indeed it was the exigencies of empire that persuaded the Coalition Cabinet of David Lloyd George to issue, on November 2, 1917, through the otherwise lucid pen of Arthur Balfour, that vaguest of all diplomatic documents, the Balfour Declaration. The British were persuaded of the validity of the proposition so often demonstrated in history, that the control of Egypt (and hence the Suez Canal) could only be secured through a glacis in Syria (geographic Syria). The high command had anticipated the day when Egypt would finally disengage itself from British control. The creation, therefore, of a "friendly" power would serve as a safeguard to British interests. But as often happens, things did not work according to plan. As the colloquial Arabic proverb says, "The estimate in the field did not match the result on the threshing-floor." What was intended as a friendly ally has turned out to be a threat to the interests of its authors.

5. Antonius, pp. 372-74.

6. Muhammad Rif'at, *al-Tayyarat al-Siyasiyyah fi Hawd al-Bahr al-Mutawassit*, Cairo, 1949, pp. 172-80.

7. Afred Bonne, *State and Economics in the Middle East: A Society in Transition*, London, 1948, pp. 284-85.

8. "Qanun Da'awi al-'Ashair al-Madaniyyah w-al-Jaza'iyyah li-Sanat 1922." This law was enacted for the purpose of securing a speedy settlement for civil and criminal cases among members of the tribes in accordance with tribal law and practice. After the occupation of Basrah in 1916, the British enacted the so-called *Bayan al-'Asha'ir* (the tribal proclamation or code), and after the occupation of Bagdad the system was extended to all the occupied parts of Iraq. The law regulating civil and criminal cases

among the tribes was issued on August 27, 1918. It was first amended on September 28, 1924, and again on June 1, 1933. It is still in force today.

9. *Qanun Huquq wa-Wajibat al-Zurra'*.

10. *Qanun al-Lizmah*. "The freehold title, described as Lazma, was a new legal category, supposedly suitable for tribal conditions. It grants freehold ownership, that is 'Tapu' title, to the occupier after ten years' cultivation as a leaseholder, and its special feature is that land so granted cannot be sold outside the tribe. The object of introducing this new type of tenure was to maintain tribal solidarity, but has not in fact had this effect, and has been mainly used by the pump owners to secure ownership against the customary rights of the tribesmen" (Doreen Warriner, *Land and Poverty in the Middle East*, London, 1948, p. 111).

11. Recent developments in Anglo-Egyptian relations concerning the Sudan, namely the agreement between the government of General Mohammed Najib and the British government for holding Sudanese elections under international supervision and the actual outcome of these elections, do not in any way affect this study. The elections were held during the fall of 1953 and resulted in a decisive victory for the anti-British parties.

12. Nicola Ziadeh, *Libya wa-Tunus wa-'l-Jaza'ir*, Beirut, 1952, pp. 25, 49-50.

13. General Augustin Guillaume, "The French Accomplishment in Morocco," in *Foreign Affairs*, XXX, No. 4 (July, 1952), 625-36.

14. *Ibid.*, pp. 633-34.

15. *Ibid.*, pp. 627, 635.

VIII. Religious Minorities

1. Before Iraq could gain admission to the League of Nations, it had to reiterate, in the so-called Declaration of 1932, these special privileges of the religious minorities, although they were already safeguarded in the Iraqi constitution of 1925.

2. A pamphlet of thirty-nine pages entitled *S. O. S. The Lebanon the "Christian National Home" of the Near East* was anonymously published sometime in 1945. It bears no date or place of publication, but was probably printed in Canada.

IX. National Minorities

1. The most recent estimates give the number of the Kurds as follows: 800,000 in Iraq, 1,500,000 in Turkey, 600,000 in Iran, 250,000 in Syria, and 20,000 in Soviet Armenia (*The Middle East*, p. 59).

2. A. H. Hourani, *Minorities in the Arab World*, London, 1947, pp. 96-98.

3. "From 1932 to 1943 the Kurds did not revolt again, but continued to be restless and unwilling to accept the authority of the Government. There were two main reasons for their restlessness. The first was the growth of the Kurdish national spirit, due partly to the gradual appearance of a class of educated Kurds, partly to a natural reaction against Pan-Arabism. The encouragement given by the French to Kurdish nationalism in the Syrian Jazirah, and by the Russians to Kurdish autonomy in the Caucasus, may have had a certain although a limited influence. The second and more fundamental reason was to be found in the particular administrative grievances of the Kurdish tribes" (Hourani, p. 98).

4. For the text of this article see *The Treaties of Peace 1919-1923*, Carnegie Endowment for International Peace, New York, 1924, II, 807-8.

5. See p. 102.

6. This method is fully illustrated in the march of al-Glawi Pasha of Marrakech and his Berber horde against Sidi Mohammed bin Youssef, the Sultan of Morocco, on February 20, 1951; by al-Glawi's instigation, on May 29, 1953, of a petition, signed by 276 Moroccans, mostly Berbers, requesting the abdication of the Sultan; and

by al-Glawi's second petition, on August 3, 1953, signed by 356 pashas, also mostly Berber, which finally led to the overthrow of the Sultan on August 20, 1953. All these were staged at the behest of the French when they discovered that Sidi Mohammed bin Youssef was no longer a docile puppet.

X. DIVERSITY OF POLITICAL AIMS

1. The first and only Copt ever to become premier in Egypt.

2. Several times prime minister. He presided over the accession and abdication of Faruq.

3. *Al-Ahram,* November 15, 1952.

4. *Ibid.,* October 11, 1952.

5. Asad Rustum and Fu'ad Afram al-Bustani, *Ta'rikh Lubnan al-Mujaz,* 2nd ed., Beirut, 1937.

6. George Sarton, "The Unity and Diversity of the Mediterranean World," *Osiris,* II, pt. 9 (September, 1936), 407-8.

7. Henri Pirenne, *Mahomet et Charlemagne,* 7th ed., Brussels, 1935.

8. For a detailed investigation of the Arabs and the Culture of the Mediterranean Basin, see Nabih Amin Faris, *al-'Arab al-Ahya',* Beirut, 1947, pp. 20-38.

9. See *Mabadi' al-Hizb* ("The Basic Principles of the Party").

10. The decisive battle against the Byzantines (636) which won Syria for the Arabs.

11. *Al-Nizam al-Jadid,* Series 12, October, 1950, p. 38.

12. *Al-'Urubah Bayn Du'atiha wa-Mu'aridiha,* pp. 73-74.

13. "Aflasat al-'Urubah," in *al-Nizam al-Jadid,* Series 12, p. 9.

14. *Ibid.,* p. 10.

15. In a special memorandum submitted to the Egyptian government requesting permission to resume their activities, the Ikhwan al-Muslimun declared, "Whereas the Ikhwan al-Muslimun, in accordance with their organic law, constitute a catholic Islamic society committed to the task of realizing the aims for which Islam was revealed, they aspire to fulfill all the aims set forth by Islam. These comprise all the affairs of life, including the trivial and the important in the life of the individual and the community. Islam makes no distinction between state and religion, and does not separate this life from the hereafter. On the contrary, Islam is at once a religion, a state, a ritual, and a military service. God has ordained that this religion be accepted in its entirety making it an indivisible whole. It is unlawful, therefore, to believe in one part and reject another, to accept one part and reject another, to accept one part and to neglect another. 'Will ye believe in one part of the Book and disbelieve in the other? Verily the reward of those who would do that among you is ignominy in this life, and on the Day of Resurrection they shall be committed to extreme torture' " *(Surah* II:85). Published in *al-Ahram,* October 9, 1952.

16. *Al-Ahram,* November 20, 1952.

17. Cited above, p. 153, note 15.

18. *Al-Ahram,* October 9, 1952. The same ideas are expressed in the old program of the Ikhwan. See Ishaq Musa al-Husayni, *al-Ikhwan al-Muslimun,* Beirut, 1952, pp. 68-69.

19. "Mabadi' al-'Alam al-Hurr," *al-Risalah,* No. 1018 (January 1, 1953). See, also, Ahmad Hasan al-Zayyat, "al-Jami'ah al-Islamiyyah Hiya 'l-Ghayah," *ibid.,* No. 730 (June 30, 1947), and 'Ali al-Tantawi, "al-'Arabiyyah w-al-Islamiyyah," *ibid.,* No. 1019 (January 12, 1953).

XI. DISPARITY IN POLITICAL DEVELOPMENT

1. On March 30, 1955, the Anglo-Iraqi Treaty of 1930 was terminated and replaced by a Mutual Defense Pact for a period of five years. Britain would still enjoy the use of all Iraqi air, land, and sea facilities in time of war. Its troops will evacuate the two air bases within a period of eleven months from the date of the agreement.

NOTES

XIII. CULTURAL DISPARITY

1. For the extent of the disparity in the educational systems of the Arab countries, see Roderic D. Matthews and Matta Akrawi, *Education in the Arab Countries of the Near East*, Washington, 1949; Sati' al-Husari, *Hawliyyat al-Thaqafah al-'Arabiyyah*, Cairo, 1949.

2. During the school year 1949-1950, Tunisians of school age numbered 600,000. Places for only 134,000 were found in government schools. In other words, only one out of every four was able to receive primary schooling, while the others were sentenced, as it were, to illiteracy and ignorance. Of those for whom there were places, 25,896 were French. Secondary-school population numbered 10,576, of whom 5,191 were French. Students in technical schools numbered 10,195, of whom 3,351 were French. Students in higher institutions of learning numbered 702, of whom 143 were French. French students made up over 22 per cent of the aggregate number of students in government schools, although the French in Tunisia were only 5 per cent of the total population. In Algeria, the total number of students for the same year, both male and female, was 212,572, of whom 138,382 were French. This represents a ratio of three Algerians to every two French students, although the ratio in the population is six to one in favor of the Algerians. The number of Algerians of school age for the same year was estimated at 1,000,000, but only one out of every four could find a place in government schools. All French children of school age in Algeria, however, were accommodated. See Ziadeh, pp. 31-32, 62-63.

3. *Hawliyyat al-Thaqafah,* p. 196.

4. Iraq Ministry of Education, *Annual Report,* 1950-1951 (Arabic), p. 3.

5. *Hawliyyat al-Thaqafah,* pp. 74, 194, 312, 356; Iraq Ministry of Education, *Annual Report,* 1950-1951, p. 2.

6. Noticeable though small progress has been made by women in some parts of the Arab world during the last three decades, particularly in Lebanon, Syria, Egypt, and Iraq. This progress has been limited to the larger cities. If the Arab world is considered in its entirety, however, the situation remains far from satisfactory.

XIV. CONCLUSION

1. Alfred Lilienthal, *What Price Israel*, Chicago, 1953, pp. 191-212.

2. C. K. Zurayk, *al-Qadiyyah al-'Arabiyyah*, Beirut, 1953.

Index

187

189